INT **ONAL**
CHRISTIAN

INTENTIONAL CHRISTIAN

CHRISTIAN

WHAT *to* DO WHEN YOU DON'T KNOW WHAT *to* DO

DANIEL RYAN DAY

Discovery House.
from Our Daily Bread Ministries

Discovery House is affiliated with Our Daily Bread Ministries,
Grand Rapids, Michigan.

Requests for permission to quote from this book should be directed to: Permissions Department, Discovery House, P.O. Box 3566, Grand Rapids, MI 49501, or contact us by e-mail at permissionsdept@dhp.org.

Interior design by Beth Shagene

Library of Congress Cataloging-in-Publication Data

Names: Day, Daniel Ryan, author.
Title: Intentional Christian : what to do when you don't know what to do / Daniel Ryan Day.
Description: Grand Rapids : Discovery House, 2017. | Includes bibliographical references.
Identifiers: LCCN 2017004445 | ISBN 9781627075947
Subjects: LCSH: Vocation—Christianity. | God (Christianity)—Will.
Classification: LCC BV4740 .D36 2017 | DDC 248.4—dc23
LC record available at https://lccn.loc.gov/2017004445

Printed in the United States of America

First printing in 2017

To my friend and mentor Robert Brenner,
who taught me that life is not about
having all of the answers
but is about walking faithfully with God.

—◇—

CONTENTS

PART 3: SPECIFIC CALLINGS

When You Don't Know What to Do

If you can force your heart and nerve and sinew
To serve your turn long after they are gone,
And so hold on when there is nothing in you
Except the Will which says to them: "Hold on!"
—Rudyard Kipling, "If"

"What are you going to do with your life? Will it matter?" I stared at the computer screen as the video continued to promise me the direction I desperately needed. I was in college, and I was tangled in braided fishing line. Not literally, of course! I was sitting at my computer searching through a tangled mess of degree options.

The time to choose a major had come, and I was days away from having to decide my degree path—to "declare" what my life would be about for the foreseeable future. There were so many options—good options—and I could see myself thriving in multiple areas of study. That's what I mean by a "tangled mess." It wasn't that the website was disorganized. In fact, Appalachian State had created an easy-to-use system to search the benefits of each college of study within the university.

The decision to choose a major was a "tangled mess" because of me. I couldn't decide what I wanted to do. By completing my general education classes first, I had spent the previous year and a half avoiding the inevitable decision to declare a major. I had hoped that by putting off the decision I would buy enough time to figure out what I wanted to do with my life. But that didn't happen. And now it was time to register for the specialized courses related to my major—a major I didn't have.

The more I searched the registrar's website and considered different options, the more confused I became. I would read about a degree option, get excited, and write it down in my composition notebook as a possibility. I would then read about another major, see potential, and mark it down as another intriguing opportunity. After a few hours of searching the website and listing degree options, I gazed hopelessly at my tangled mess of promising majors. I simply did not know what to do.

As a culture, we place a lot of pressure on high school and college students to figure out the rest of their lives when they are very young—especially as it relates to choosing an occupation. As a result, we are left with over-stressed teenagers, major-less college students, and many young adults (and some adults in their 30s and 40s even) who bounce from job to job trying to figure out the answer to the question: What am I supposed to do with my life? That night in college—in the midst of considering numerous majors—I sensed that pressure.

Because of the pressure to figure out the rest of my life, I felt paralyzed by all of the options. I was almost in a daze, and that night I lost the ability to consider the differences among all the opportunities. I was no longer able to make decisions. Do you know that feeling—the feeling of weighing the pros and cons of a decision, any decision, for so long that you can no longer analyze things clearly?

I left the university website and began surfing the web. I ended up on Facebook, and I noticed that a friend had posted a link to a video. I clicked on the link.

"What are you going to do with your life?" a voice asked. "Will it matter?" The video went on to describe a leadership institute in Colorado that could help me discover the answers I was looking for. I was sold. Finally, after a confusing year and a half of searching for the right major, I had stumbled across something that seemed to offer the answers I was looking for. I don't remember what the rest of the video was about, but I was ready to sign up for whatever could help me figure out how to "discover my calling" and begin living a life that mattered.

I wish I could tell you I discovered all the answers I was looking for, but perhaps you can already guess how this story went. The institute was great, but after six months in Colorado I found myself tangled in the same mess I had been in that night at Appalachian State University.

Maybe you too have been in a situation where you didn't know what to do. Perhaps the decision had nothing to do with choosing a major or settling on a career, but it was an important decision, and you felt pressure to choose the right option. Where did you go to find answers? Maybe instead of attending a leadership institute, you read a book about calling, attended a class on a subject you were interested in, traveled somewhere new and exciting, or met with a recruiter who promised direction for your life.

Regardless of what path you chose, I wonder if you found all the answers you were looking for. I wonder if that direction—the one the book, class, location, or recruiter provided—answered all the deepest longings of your heart.

Indeed, there are moments in our lives when we simply don't know what to do:

- when we are faced with decisions about the future,
- when tragedy strikes,
- when our faith journey seems static, or
- when we experience a life-change such as going to college, having a child, or moving to a different state.

Sometimes we are presented with several good options, but we don't know which to choose. At other times we don't have any options, and we feel trapped. Either way, not knowing what to do can be tough.

Uncertainty can be even more difficult when things don't work out the way we expect them to—maybe there's a relationship breakup, we are blindsided by a layoff at work, or we fail a required class.

Not too long ago, my sister-in-law Maggie found out that her college was closing—and she was just one year away from graduation. Instead of completing her degree at the school she had chosen three years earlier—a school she had grown to love—she suddenly had to transfer somewhere else. I remember vividly the questions she struggled with: "Where will I go? Will my credits transfer so I can finish on time? Will I have to move to another state? Will I ever see my friends again? Why did God let this happen to me?"

Think about it. Maggie had already gone through the emotional struggle many of us have experienced: the struggle of searching for the right college, the discovery of what she thought God wanted for her, and the commitment to the school of her dreams. Suddenly, through no fault of her own, her college experience—and her life—came to a screeching halt. The bridge to graduation had collapsed, and she had no idea how to get to the other side of what appeared to be a canyon-sized gap between where she was and the elusive degree she was pursuing.

There was no solution in sight for Maggie. All her expectations, along with her understanding of her life's direction, plummeted to the bottom of an inescapable chasm.

I'm guessing that most people who have found themselves in a situation where life takes an unexpected turn have felt this way—as if life itself is on hold. Or worse: it is spiraling out of control.

A few years ago, I too experienced a painful time of uncertainty. I was a few weeks away from the release of my first book, *Ten Days Without*, and I had been invited to speak at an event in Michigan. My wife and I were so excited! A lifelong dream of mine—the dream to publish a book—had come true, and I couldn't wait to engage with an audience around the content I had written.

The Michigan trip would be the first stop in a month-long book tour, and I had already set up a few more speaking gigs in the Southeast. Rebecca and I decided to bring the whole family and use the time in between speaking engagements as a much-needed vacation. In fact, just a few days before the event in Michigan, we stopped in Chicago for our first visit to Navy Pier, the Chicago Discovery Children's Museum, and the Great Lakes. The tour was off to a killer start!

Finally, the time came for my first presentation, and my speech went almost exactly as I had expected. Although there were fewer people in the audience than I had hoped, I hit all of the points I wanted to cover. Emotionally, I was floating. Getting to speak about the book I had written was even better than I had anticipated. The moment I was finished, I knew I had nailed it! If there hadn't still been people in the room—or if I had been equipped with a cone of silence—I would have shouted something equivalent to "THAT. WAS. AWESOME!"

A few moments later, after everyone else had left the room, my boss—who was also in town speaking at the event—congratulated me and told me I had done an excellent job. He told me I communicated each point clearly, and he said the content was going to really help a lot of people. He told me he was glad he got to see the talk, because he knew I'd be okay.

And then he fired me!

I was completely blindsided ... and in shock.

Talk about an emotional swing! I went from the top of the top to a very low low. What was I going to do now?

I walked out of the ballroom and into the greenroom, where my wife was playing with the kids. As soon as she saw my face, she knew something was wrong.

"Oh, no! What happened? What went wrong?" she asked. She expected me to tell her that my computer crashed in the middle of the presentation, that I had forgotten what to say, or that I had told a joke in the presentation that completely bombed. My response stunned her.

"Well, uh, I don't have a job anymore," I said solemnly.

The next few weeks did not go as expected—for me or for

my wife. Remember, we were in Michigan, and we had *driven* there with three small children. We were fifteen hours away from our home in Colorado. We didn't know if we should cancel the book tour and drive back to our house, or if we should try to keep going.

My family was thirteen hours away in North Carolina, and we both thought it sounded good to go somewhere where we could have support. We figured that being near family would be the best place to begin trying to figure out what was next. So we drove to North Carolina. As you can probably imagine, it was a long thirteen hours. We were hurt, we were angry, and we had no idea what we would do next.

The only bright spot of that infamous night was when we stopped at a coffee shop to load up on caffeine before the long drive to North Carolina. It was Halloween night, and the lady behind the counter gave all three of our kids a free hot chocolate since they had missed their opportunity to trick-or-treat.

All of us have been in situations where we didn't know what to do next. Not all of those scenarios are as painful as the one I just described, but each of us is searching for, has searched for, or will search for the answers to the questions: "What am I supposed to do with my life?" And "Will it matter?"

I'm not writing this book as an expert on the will of God for your life but as a fellow sojourner attempting to figure out why God has me on this planet called Earth. And as we begin this journey, it's important to recognize that we are in this together. As a result, I hope you will treat this as a conversation and not a lecture.

In fact, I welcome the chance to go back and forth with

you on this topic—and I hope you will use the opportunities provided by Amazon and Facebook to let me know what you think (i.e., reviews, comments, etc.). My guess is that God will use you to help me and other readers come to a more complete understanding of the purpose of life. To share your thoughts, visit facebook.com/danielryanday; follow the conversation on Twitter @danielryanday; or write a review on Amazon. I'm eager and excited to hear from you!

God has already used some really wise people to teach me some really cool things about the idea of a "calling" in life—ideas I think many people have missed. I'll share those things with you as we go along. I hope you will get to the end of this book and know exactly what you should do next, even if you don't know for sure what you should do for the rest of your life.

As we work our way through the book, I will be outlining the ideas that have helped me. But this doesn't mean you and I will be satisfied with where we end up. I'm not. The purpose of this book is not to provide all the answers but to help us take a few more steps down the road to discovering God's calling on our lives.

An old saying by Ralph Waldo Emerson suggests that each point along a journey, our journey, can be its own end, which may be a good way for us to judge the next eleven chapters of our conversation. Emerson wrote, "To finish the moment, to find the journey's end in every step of the road ... is wisdom."[1] In other words, if you and I can take a few steps down the road to figuring out what life is about, those steps are a few victories in the journey, and they are the milestones we can look back on and build on. Rabbi Alvin Fine says it this way: "We see that victory lies not at some high place along the way, but in having made the journey, stage by stage.... Life is a journey, a sacred pilgrimage to life everlasting."[2]

So I ask you: Will you join me on a journey to explore this question:

What am I supposed to do with my life?

PART 1

SOMETHING IS WRONG

CHAPTER ONE

When This Whole "Dream Job" Thing Isn't Working Out

Two roads diverged in a yellow wood,
And sorry I could not travel both
And be one traveler, long I stood
And looked down one as far as I could
To where it bent in the undergrowth.

—ROBERT FROST, "The Road Not Taken"

There's a toy airplane on my desk in my office at home. It's a biplane made of tin, and my boys bought it for me for Christmas a few years ago. They bought it because they love airplanes, and I think they saw an opportunity to have a "toy-in-disguise" in Daddy's office. But what they may not have realized is how much their daddy loves airplanes too.

When I was a boy, I thought for sure I would fly F-16s when I grew up. It's all I wanted to do with my life. I was so serious about it that I built control panels out of Legos, "borrowed" the joystick from my parent's computer, and set up my bed as the cockpit of one of those amazing machines. I would sit on my bed and fly thousands of missions all over the world. I don't mean to brag, but I was the best fighter pilot ever to fly a four-banister bed.

As I got older, my desire to fly airplanes grew stronger. When I turned seventeen, I contacted my congressman, and he agreed to write a recommendation letter for my acceptance into the United States Air Force Academy. Unless you're a really bad student with a criminal record, a letter from a congressman almost always guarantees acceptance into the Academy. So I was set.

Before I sent in my application, however, I met a cute little Cuban girl who stole my heart. The thought of moving to Colorado to attend the Air Force Academy instead of being close to Rebecca sounded terrible, so I never sent in the application. Instead, I went to a local university, and Rebecca and I were married a few years later.

My desire to fly, however, never went away. In fact, a few months before our wedding, I met with an Air Force recruiter to check out the process of becoming a pilot without going through the Academy. Providentially, he was a terrible recruiter, and I left my meeting with him confused and without any peace about the possibility of becoming an Air Force pilot.

I tried a different route. I contacted my uncle, who had flown missionary planes for the Jungle Aviation and Radio Service (JAARS) for close to fifty years. He advised me about what it would take to become a missionary pilot, and soon I was accepted by a university that specialized in the type of training I would need. By this time, I was married, and my wife was ready to follow me wherever I needed to go. But again, just like what had happened when I left the recruiter's office, I didn't feel peace about this decision. Instead of changing colleges, I finished my business degree at the local university at which I had begun.

For most of my college and early adult life, I wondered if I had missed "it"—my dream job. Flying sounded so adventurous and exciting! The idea of watching the sun rise and set from high above the earth sounded so beautiful, amazing, and special. It sounded like the perfect dream job. In fact, over the next few years whenever another job became difficult or stressful, I felt a burning in my chest to abandon everything and jump into a cockpit. Over time, I got to the point where I felt that if I didn't become a pilot, I could never be content in another job.

To this day, a welling up of energy rises within me whenever I think about flying airplanes. However, I'm now 100 percent certain that I'm not supposed to become a professional pilot. I have lost all desire to go into the Air Force. But there's still a part of me that loves looking at the tin biplane on my desk and dreaming about what it would be like to fly for real.

DREAM JOBS

What is your absolute "dream job"? I'm not talking about your *practical* dream job—the one that would be nice and that you might be able to get. I'm talking about your no-holds-barred, money-is-not-an-issue, genie-in-a-bottle dream job. The job you are sure would bring you more excitement and energy than you've ever enjoyed. The job that wouldn't even feel like a job but like a fulltime vacation. The job that would rock your socks off every day and bring in ridiculous amounts of money. Can you picture it?

Right now, I manage a family entertainment center and a hotel. We employ a hundred or so people, and they all seem to be looking for their dream jobs. The majority of our staff falls into the category of people "in transition." Many know exactly what their dream jobs are, but many others have absolutely no idea. And it's not just the young adults. I also work with men and women in their twenties, thirties, and older who are searching for something better—a job both fulfilling and exciting. These folks are looking for a dream job, but they are having a hard time finding it.

Consider Andrew, for example. He was one of the key managers at our fun center, but he was always searching for something more. He and I talked often about his desire to do something different, but he was having a hard time figuring out what he should do. The harder he tried to figure it out, the less content he was to work at the fun center. Eventually, it got to the point where I had to confront him about his obvious lack of enthusiasm for his job.

"Okay, Andrew," I began, "I can tell that you are no longer happy working here, that you're frustrated and stressed out. What's up? Is there anything I can do for you? I want to help, man. I like having you around."

"Well, uh," Andrew started hesitantly, "as you know, I've been here a long time, and it's not that I don't like the job—there are a lot of things I like about it. But there are a lot of things I want to accomplish with my life, and I don't think I can do that here."

"Okay. I can understand that. What do you want to accomplish? Maybe there's something I can do to help you get there."

"Well, I want to race cars. I've always wanted to race, and I'm pretty good at it. My dream has always been to join a racing circuit and get sponsored."

For obvious reasons, I wasn't able to help Andrew. I would have done whatever I could to help him reach his goals, but the closest things I had to racecars were video games and go-carts. Both are super fun, but they weren't going to prepare Andrew to join a racing circuit.

A few months after our conversation, Andrew left our company and became a mailman. He's now spending more time on the road, but he's still not living his dream. My guess is that he'll eventually end up in the same frustrated and discouraged state he was in when we talked about his dream of driving racecars. I think that's a good guess, because I've experienced the same frustration.

WHAT EVERYONE WANTS (OR AT LEAST WHAT I WANT)

After working with so many people "in transition," I've become convinced of something. Although our definitions of a "dream job" may differ, all of us have this in common: We all want to thrive in our jobs and in our lives. Our definitions of what it means to thrive may differ, but most people I know think thriving means finding purpose and fulfillment in all they do, including their jobs. See if you agree with me.

Purpose

First, in order to thrive, we need to feel a sense of purpose. Very simply, we want to know that we are on the right road. We want to know that if we walk down a particular road and accomplish the things we are meant to accomplish, then our lives will matter. All of us long to know that there's a reason behind our existence—that our lives are in some way important.

Don't you? Don't you want your life to mean something? Don't you want to know you are on the right path and you are accomplishing all the things you are meant to accomplish? I know I do.

This world is a big place, and we share it with a lot of people. Think about a time when you've been in an airplane at night, flying over a city. It doesn't matter if it was a big city or a small town, within a period of just a few moments the lives of multitudes of people flash before your eyes. It can be captivating to look down and think about how each streetlight or house light or car light glittering in the night represents someone's existence. During that nighttime flight, did you stop for a moment to think about the fact that his or her life is a lot like yours, yet in a completely different context?

For this very reason, every time I fly I hope to be in a window seat. I like to look down and imagine the stories:

> "Maybe the people in that car are driving to a fast-food restaurant for a late-night snack."
>
> "I wonder if those people are taking a trip to the grocery store to pick up diapers."
>
> "Oops! That person just got pulled over. I wonder how fast he or she was going."

Whatever I see going on below me, I'm always mesmerized by the fact that I just witnessed light after light and life after life in just a few minutes.

I'm also amazed at the size of the world in which we live.

This is a *big* place! And the more technologically advanced we become, the more we get to witness the size of the world. I think this may lead us to struggle more intensely with our desire to matter. We want to know that our lives mean something, that our existence in the world is part of a bigger plan, and that we are accomplishing something great. We want to know we are special and important to our families and friends. We want to know that our jobs—jobs that often take up a large portion of our waking hours—are not just pawns in the grand scheme of a massive world economy. We want to believe that the tasks to which we dedicate our lives make a difference in the world.

We long to matter and to make a difference, and these desires shape the search for our dream job. Although we may not go as far as to say we don't care about how much money we make, or if our jobs are marked by action and adventure, most all of us want our everyday tasks to affect the world in a positive way. In other words, when it comes to finding a dream job, we're all looking for a sense of purpose.

Fulfillment

Second, when it comes to defining our own dream jobs, all of us want to enjoy some level of fulfillment. I don't think I've ever talked to anyone who doesn't want to enjoy his or her work and achieve some level of accomplishment and fulfillment.

Most people I've talked with seem to have a desire to enjoy their jobs. As I've talked with members of my staff, I've heard many different definitions of what it means to enjoy work. Some want to experience adventure, while others want to care for children, create or capture beauty, or compete at the highest levels of a sport.

Along with a sense of enjoyment, most people would likely say that finding fulfillment in their work also means feeling a sense of accomplishment. Yet accomplishment, like enjoyment, looks different for different people. Some people are all about the cash and want to reach a high level of wealth. Others, however, couldn't care less about money and would find fulfillment in knowing they are helping people.

What about you? Do you want to enjoy purpose and fulfillment in your work and in your life? Do you want to enjoy going to work while also knowing that you are accomplishing something great? I think for most of us, the answer to those questions is obviously yes! I know it is for me. I want to find and enjoy a fulfilling job. Is this really too much to ask? It just might be!

WHEN THE "DREAM JOB" MEETS REALITY

Although we all might want some of the same things out of a job, not all of us are searching for the same type of dream job. My buddy Andrew was looking for a job that would allow him to experience the pleasure of driving a car on the very edge of control. His definition of a dream job is pretty specific: he wants to drive fast, compete at a high level, and win. Yet Andrew can't find his dream job, and because of that, he can't see any way to accomplish what he wants to do with his life.

Like Andrew, a lot of people I know would define their dream job as one marked with adventure and adrenaline. I think I've defined most of my dream jobs this way. I already mentioned I once wanted to be a fighter pilot, but that is only one of the many "dream jobs" I've pursued. When my dream of becoming a pilot didn't work out, I started looking for another adventurous occupation. At one point, I almost followed in my uncle's footsteps and became an FBI agent. At the time, all I could think about was how cool it would be to get in gunfights and catch bad guys.

One day, my uncle took me to his office so I could see what it was like to save the world as a crimefighter. He is very proud of his job with the FBI, and it excited him that someone else in the family showed interest. I too was excited! I couldn't wait to wear a bulletproof vest while interviewing incarcerated informants in locked interrogation rooms. I wondered who we might interrogate first. In fact, I began to think of what questions my uncle may need *me* to ask. Maybe I would be the good cop, and he would be the bad cop—sorry, *agent*. Or maybe it would be reversed, and he would be the good agent and I would be the bad agent. I began to imagine how epic it would feel to slam a bad guy's forehead into the desk to get him to talk. I hoped I was strong enough to knock the truth out of him.

When we walked into my uncle's office, though, I was surprised to find that it looked like ... well, like an office. He had a desk, a computer, paper, and pens. There wasn't a gun range, and there weren't guns hanging on the walls. There weren't interrogation rooms with one-way-mirrors, gray lamps, and metal tables. Instead, there was a conference room with a wooden table, executive chairs, and the spaceship-looking thingy that helps with conference calls. I was even more surprised to discover that my uncle did a lot of his investigations from his desk—I'm serious—with just his phone and his computer. What? No red phone that calls the Oval Office directly? No secret lever on the bookshelf that opens up a wall revealing a hidden gunroom filled with exotic weapons?

When I pictured my life as an FBI agent, I didn't see an office job. I envisioned going with my uncle to pick up the modern-day version of mobster Benjamin "Bugsy" Siegel, and then I wanted to interrogate him into giving up the location of his boss. Or maybe we would run into Charles "Lucky" Luciano's barber and discover that if we raced to the docks, we would catch him in the act of doing something *really* bad—like smuggling narcotics into the country by hiding them inside teddy bears. My uncle wouldn't have time to drop me off with my parents, and I would end up on the front page of *The New York Times* as the "everyman" (I mean "-boy") who was there when Lucky's luck ran out.

Although we can see these kinds of scenes in old gangster movies, that was far from my uncle's reality. I lost interest in the FBI that day. I didn't want to do office work; I wanted to live on the edge.

I think a lot of people want that. And many of us have a hard time finding a job that gets us anywhere close to the edge.

But that's not for everyone. My college friend Ben enjoys action and adventure, but he wouldn't define his dream job that way. Instead, he would define his dream job as one that allows him to research stock markets and build wealth for himself and for others. He's not all about the cash, but his dream job is directly related to managing people's portfolios.

When we were in college, I walked into Ben's dorm room one day to find him reading a book on stocks. When I asked him what class it was for, he told me: "It's not for a class, I just like researching how the markets work." *Really?* I thought. *Who does that?*

Ben knew what his dream job was, but boy did he struggle to get there! After college, he bounced from job to job. He did everything he could to make his dream of becoming a financial planner a reality, but several years went by as he searched for his opportunity. Finally, a promising spot with a premier company opened up, and Ben applied and was accepted. Everything was great! He had finally reached his dream, and it was even better than he had imagined. I remember calling him at one time, and he told me he was at the beach with his wife for a training seminar. I think they were staying at a Hilton—right on the water—and all of their meals were paid for.

A few months later, however, Ben called me to let me know his portfolio had fallen one account shy of making the cut, and he had been fired from his dream job. Here was a guy who got close to exactly what he wanted, and then his dream job slipped away. Ben didn't care about action and adventure; he wanted to help people with their finances. Unfortunately, that job was hard to find too.

I know other people who don't care so much about action or money, but instead are looking for a job that allows them to express themselves. Many of the people I work with long to be photographers, actors, graphic artists, or musicians. Although all of us probably have a desire to express who we really are in the work we do, these people would *define* their dream jobs with this desire in mind. I don't know if you've noticed it, but there are a lot of aspiring photographers, actors, graphic artists, and musicians working in coffee shops, at bookstores, or at family entertainment centers. That's mostly because it's extremely difficult to find steady work in the more "artistic" fields.

I can think of one other group that would have a specific definition of a dream job—those who are fighting for a cause. Many who fight for a cause couldn't care less about money, and some give up everything to stand firm on their convictions.

I'm reminded of the White House Peace Vigil started by William Thomas in 1981. It's called the "*White House* Peace Vigil" because it was started outside of the presidential mansion in Washington, D. C. Thomas silently protested nuclear arms by setting up a tent near the back gate of the White House and by propping anti-nuclear escalation signs against the canvas.

As a result of Thomas's protest, a Spanish woman named Concepcion Picciotto (later called Connie) started camping near the back gate of the White House with him. Their protest has been called the longest running anti-war protest in US history.[1] William camped outside the White House for twenty-eight years, until his death in 2009. Connie died in 2016 after thirty-five years of living in a tent near the White House. If you have ever visited the presidential mansion in Washington, D.C. you have likely seen their tents—still up—near the back entrance of the White House. Regardless of whether or not you agree with them, William and Connie gave up everything for the cause. Their dream job was living out their passion for what they felt was a vital cause.

How would you define your specific dream job? Have you found it yet? Or are you still searching for it? Are you looking for action and adventure like I was? Do you want to help others achieve success? Do you want to support and stand for a cause?

Maybe you've read this chapter up to this point, and you realize you can't answer these questions because you don't yet know what your dream job looks like. Now, that's frustrating!

I too have experienced the frustration of not being able to answer what seems to be a simple series of questions. After neither of my youthful dreams—becoming a pilot or catching bad guys with the FBI—worked out, I struggled to find something else that excited me. My friends tried to help, but I found their questions more annoying than helpful:

"What do you *want* to do?"

"I don't know," I would reply.

"What are your passions?"

"I don't know."

"If you could close your eyes and picture the perfect job, what would it be?"

"I DON'T KNOW!"

These seem like simple questions, and it made me feel silly to think that I didn't know myself well enough to have the answers. But I didn't *have* answers, so I couldn't give a reply when my friends asked these questions.

If you are at that same point in your life—feeling frustrated because you can't answer these same questions—you can take comfort in knowing that you're not alone. I've been there myself. It's frustrating to not know what to do and to not be able to get where you want to go.

All of the scenarios in this chapter are real-life situations that represent the struggles many of us deal with at one time or another. Maybe you can see yourself in several of these stories, or maybe you can identify with only one. But regardless of which story hits home, I think a lot of us are frustrated because we can't land that dream job our culture tells us we should pursue.

The dream job search can be maddening—regardless of what category you fall into. You might feel frustrated because your dreams feel impractical. Or perhaps you really have no idea what you want to do. Maybe you have several good options, but none of them fits with what you want to do. Or maybe you're looking at the job market and see so many potential career paths that you're paralyzed by the weight of opportunity. Regardless of where you are in your search, the search for your dream job can be frustrating. Many are either tempted to give up or have already done so.

So let me ask you: Where are you on this journey? Did you pick up this book because you still hope you can figure it out? Or are you reading this book as a last-ditch effort to stumble into the perfect job you've missed up to this point? No matter your situation, come along with me as we look at some ideas I hope will help you in this all-important search.

CHAPTER TWO

When God Won't Answer

*A hurricane wind ripped through the mountains and
shattered the rocks before God, but God wasn't to be found
in the wind; after the wind an earthquake, but God
wasn't in the earthquake; and after the earthquake fire,
but God wasn't in the fire; and after the fire . . .*
—1 Kings 19:11–12 msg

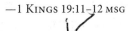

I walked upstairs into what felt like a cold cafeteria. The floor
was made of tile, the walls were painted almost white, and
the whole room felt sanitized. Come to think of it, it kind of
smelled sanitized. I guess it had just been cleaned. I was seventeen years old, and this was my first trip back to my old church
youth room. I had forgotten how cold that room could get,
and now, without the traffic light and movie posters, it seemed
colder.

My church was growing like crazy, and we had continued
to build new additions to house the influx of people. This was
great news for the youth, because we were given a brand-new
youth wing. Unlike the old youth room, with its tile and white
walls, the floors in the new youth wing were carpeted, the stage
was decked out with lights, and the lobby housed brand-new

pool and foosball tables. I love foosball! The new youth wing was awesome and so much better than the room I was in now.

After moving all of the middle and high school students to the youth wing, the church hadn't found a use for the old youth room. It was too big for Sunday school classes but too small for most church gatherings. As a result, it had sat empty for several months—until today.

Today was the first in a series of classes on the topic of "calling." By the end of the class, the pastor would lead a ceremony in which he would hand out certificates to all of the "called." You didn't have to be called to join the class. The purpose of the gathering was to consider what a "calling" looks like and to discover if you were one of the "special" people God had picked—I guess for His playground dodgeball team. I really wanted to be on the team, and so did a lot of other people. That's why the meeting had been moved upstairs. They needed more room to host all of the people who were searching for the call of God.

At the time, I was struggling to figure out what I should do with my life. I was in the process of choosing a college, and I had recently been rejected from the university of my dreams. For as long as I could remember, I had wanted to go to one particular college in North Carolina. I visited the school several times, and I even went to a few football games. I had already talked with the recruiter for the Air Force ROTC. Unfortunately, all of my desire to attend this university couldn't make up for my less-than-stellar effort in high school—and by "less-than-stellar," I mean I fell asleep in class a lot and hardly ever studied. As you can imagine, my lack of effort led to less-than-stellar grades, which led to, well, I already told you—I was rejected by the university of my dreams. As a result, I had no idea what to do next.

I was a leader in the youth group at the time, and I had attended several youth camps where the subject of "calling" had been discussed. The idea of God calling me to something special sounded pretty cool, and I figured that as a leader, I should have one—a calling, that is. So I was looking for it. My search wasn't going anywhere, however. I had been praying for God to reveal His will, but He was being pretty quiet about it. So when I heard about the calling class, I signed up immediately.

The day finally came, and I was nervous. Yet I was also excited. In just a few short weeks (or maybe today, on Day 1), God would reveal to me His plan for my life through a specialized calling. What was He going to say? Where would I be living? What would I be doing? I had no idea what to expect, but I eagerly anticipated some major answers—even if it meant sitting in a cold room for an hour or so each week.

For Christians, the search for a dream job can be even more confusing than for those outside the faith. As we talked about in chapter 1, there's a longing within us deeper than just the desire for a purposeful and fulfilling occupation—although we definitely want that too. Christians should search for God's will for their lives. After all, we believe that He *should* have something to say about our futures because, well, He's God. This means the choice of a job is not fully up to us. It's a little like a healthy marriage, this becoming a Christian. Decisions suddenly require the agreement of two entities instead of just one. In the same way a good husband wants to please his wife and a good wife her husband, good Christians should want to please God and accomplish what He wants them to accomplish.

As a result of a Christian's desire to please God, he or she will want to wait until He tells him or her what to do—especially when searching for the right job. Traditionally, this moment of hearing from God is referred to as "the call of God," and we Christians have grown up hearing *a lot* about that subject.

During my "calling" class, several church leaders, including the senior pastor, taught me that God had a special assignment for my life—something I was uniquely equipped to handle and specifically gifted to complete. They said this assignment was God's "calling" on my life, and I needed to discover this calling in order to experience true fulfillment and purpose. In other words, they merged the concepts of a dream job and the call of God.

The class emphasized being "called" to the mission field or "called" into ministry. The speakers made such a big deal out of the people who were called to ministry that it sounded as if they were somehow closer to God and more special to Him than everyone else. There were times when a pastor would say something like, "You can be at a secular job and still be in ministry," or he might suggest that "your business is your ministry," but I never really believed him. It seemed to me that my church consisted of two groups of people—the called and the uncalled, and God especially favored the called.

Consider it my human pride or my immature faith, but I wanted to be among the "called." As a result, I got to the end of the class and made it known to the leadership team that I was one of those people God spoke to—someone God *needs* on His team in order to do His real ministry here on earth. They celebrated with me, and I was presented with my official "Calling" certificate. (I think I still have it stored away somewhere.) The problem is, I didn't receive a specific calling during the class. I kind of lied about that. Is that bad? But in my mind, it was okay to tell this little fib because I was convinced that the specific calling was on its way. I believed that when God was ready for me to find out what it was, He would let me know. I just needed to be faithful and keep searching.

Unfortunately, God continued to stay rather silent on this subject long after the class ended. He never seemed to answer my repetitive pleas for the special revelation of my "it"—the purposeful and fulfilling assignment He had prepared specifically for me before the creation of the world. I would pray and seek, and seek and pray, and God would sit back and listen—*only* listen. In contrast to what the class had taught, and as far as I could tell, God had no interest in telling me His plan for my life. And the more He met my prayers with silence, the harder I tried to figure out my calling.

In some ways, the pursuit of God's calling felt like a high-stakes game of hide-and-seek, and the entire world was the playground. It was "high stakes" because I believed that I needed to discover His calling in order to be obedient to Him and please Him with my life. It was also the most expansive game of hide-and-seek I've ever played because it encompassed the entire world.

And I can promise you this: God hid my calling well—too well!

A HIDDEN CALLING

The other day, I played hide-and-seek with my kids, and I discovered an incredible hiding place. I pulled some clothes to the side in my closet, got behind them, and pulled them back in front of me. I hid so well my kids gave up and stopped looking for me. I didn't know they had quit, because I was so tired I fell asleep in the closet. I don't know how long I was asleep in the closet, but when I woke up and came out, the kids had forgotten we were playing. I found them building Legos.

I think my calling—like me—fell asleep in a closet somewhere, because even now, several years later, I'm still not quite sure where my calling is. I keep thinking that at some point it will wake up and realize I gave up and the game is over.

I truly wanted to discover my calling. I wanted to be obedient to God. But I still had no idea what I was supposed to do with my life, and God wasn't making the search any easier. I couldn't figure out why He would do that to me—why He would stay silent when I pleaded with Him for an answer. But He did. He stayed silent!

Looking back, I can now see that my expectations of how God should speak to me were based on two assumptions. First, I assumed God wanted me to find a job that was both purposeful and fulfilling. Seems like a safe assumption, right? Doesn't it make sense that God would want me to experience enjoyment and accomplishment in my work?

Second, I was keenly aware of how much time is dedicated to a job, and I also knew my life needed to be dedicated to God. As a result, I grew up assuming God's call would be directly related to what I did for a living (my dream job). Again, makes sense. Why would God have me spend forty-five hours a week doing something unrelated to His will or calling? I didn't think He would.

My two assumptions—that God wanted me to enjoy my work and that my job and calling would be related—led me to combine my desire for a dream job with my pursuit of God's call. In other words, I concluded that my dream job and my calling would be the same thing.

I could be wrong, but I don't think I'm the only person who has combined both concepts: a dream job and God's calling. I think most Christians want to find the perfect job while also pleasing God in all they do. More than that, I think we've been encouraged to combine dream jobs and calling—just as I was told to do in my calling class.

Christian culture, it seems, has capitalized on the blurring together of dream jobs and the call of God. The other day I saw an ad on a vanity publisher's website that read: "Answer God's call to publish your book." A vanity publisher is a self-publisher that provides people who dream of becoming an author with the opportunity to pay thousands of dollars to get a book published. I'm not implying there's anything wrong with selling a publishing package, but this ad plays off the assumptions we've already discussed: that a dream job and God's call will be the same thing.

In case the quote above isn't enough to convince you of the publisher's intentions, consider a recent blog on the website titled: "The Fulfillment of a Dream."[1] A woman named Jennifer had a dream to write children's books—it was her dream job. Jennifer also felt called to minister to children. Supposedly, the publisher helped her both accomplish her dream and answer the call of God … for only $2,500.

You could look at the websites of almost any Christian publisher and find similar messaging and stories.

Take a moment to do a web search for books related to discovering God's call on your life. You will find numerous titles, all of which imply that the author has discovered the one-size-fits-all formula to discovering both your dream job and the will of God. You will notice that a lot of the covers include a compass or a street sign to suggest they've found your direction—as if they've done the work and discovered the path of God for your life. Yet you and I both know there's no such formula to finding God's will.

We've read these books, but they've failed to deliver the answers we are looking for. That's why there's a broken compass on the front of this book—the ways of searching for a dream job and God's call as outlined in the products mentioned above are broken. At least they feel broken to me. After all, if one of the books I'm referring to had answered all my questions, I wouldn't have a shelf full of resources on the same topic.

It's not just publishers either. There are many Christian speakers, bloggers, and leaders who have made a lot of money convincing me—and other young people like me—to pursue our dreams, because that's what God wants for us … what He's *called* us to do. We can become so desperate to discover God's call for our lives that we buy whatever promises us the answers. I mentioned my shelf of books on the subjects of dream jobs and calling. I also have numerous podcasts on these subjects, and I have the links to several "calling" blogs saved in my browser. These leaders have blurred the lines between a dream job and the call of God, and I've bought into it.

And just in case you want a few more examples, I've compiled a list of other places where I've noticed Christian leaders combining these topics:

1. A website that helps Christians "find a calling and not just a job."[2]

2. A prominent Christian magazine that helps you discover where "God's Purpose and Your Passion Meet."[3]

3. A recent radio program titled "How to Land the Job of Your Dreams," which promises, "He [God] created your work to be more than 'just what you do for a living,' but a place to fulfill God's calling in your life."[4]

4. Websites, blogs, magazine articles, and radio programs that provide tools to help you "identify the unique assets God has given you for your dream job."[5]

DESPERATE FOR ANSWERS

We are bombarded with so many confusing messages that it's no wonder we struggle to find God's will for our lives. First, the world teaches us that we need to discover a dream job, yet with so many options, it's difficult to choose what we want to do. Second, Christians experience a higher level of pressure because we've combined the search for a dream job with the teaching that God has a unique and specialized calling for each of us. Yet none of us is very good at either discovering our dream jobs or hearing from God on this subject.

As a result, we become more and more frustrated with our inability to discover simple answers to what we feel should be simple questions: "What is my dream job?" and "What is God's calling on my life?" The longer we go without finding the answers to these simple questions, the more frustrated we get. And the more frustrated we get, the more likely our frustration will morph into desperation.

There's a meaningful quote I want to share with you—a quote that has challenged me—because I tend to do the opposite of what it teaches.

"Wise people do not do desperate things."

I wish I could say I've always lived by this principle, but that's not the case. When I get desperate for an answer to one of life's many questions, I tend to grab at whatever seems to offer a "good enough" answer.

In this chapter, I want to share with you about a time when my desperate desire to hear God's call on my life led me to, well, kind of invent a calling. I don't know if you've ever done that before, but I did, and the story is kind of embarrassing (and also kind of funny).

I grew up learning and playing multiple musical instruments. When I was eight years old, my mom enrolled me in piano lessons, and I played from then until now. In middle school, I bought my first guitar and taught myself how to play chords. Around that same time, I also learned how to play the trumpet. At one point, I learned a few chords and a few picking patterns on the banjo as well, and I also taught myself a few notes on my sister's flute. I love music, and I've played many instruments for much of my life.

More than just playing instruments, I also grew up writing

music. Specifically, I've written many worship songs to God. These songs would come out of both intimate quiet times with the Lord and out of painful life experiences. As a result, the lyrics were deeply personal. I wrote my songs down in my journal, and for a long time, I didn't share them with anyone but my parents. Looking back, this was probably wise. After all, who wants to hear a song written by an emotionally unstable middle schooler?

Over time, I felt led to write songs for friends who were going through difficult situations. Like my worship songs, these lyrics were also very personal and written for a very particular audience—normally one person or a small group of people. In other words, the songs were *not* written for a universal Christian audience but were crafted to speak to someone stuck in a specific struggle.

In high school and college, I had many opportunities to lead worship at church. During this season of my life, I became quite confident in my ability—maybe, as you will see, confident to a fault. Not only did I feel like I was pretty good but my friends also began telling me I was doing a good job (of course they did; they were my friends). Hearing all those compliments made my head start to grow (not literally, I think).

At about the same time my friends were telling me how great I was at leading worship, I began struggling to figure out what to do with my life. I was entrenched in the struggle to discover both my dream job and God's calling. This is when I attended the calling class I wrote about at the beginning of this chapter. The positive feedback and the calling class led me to wonder if it was God's will for me to pursue a career as a professional musician.

The more I thought and prayed about it, the more I noticed a pattern of coincidences that proved my hypothesis: God had created me to become a Christian rock star (in the humble worship leader sense of the term, of course). God never told me to become a rock star; I was simply taking inventory of my gifts, applying the lessons I had learned in the calling class, and drawing my own conclusions (also known as putting words in God's mouth).

First, I "heard" God tell me He wanted me to record my songs. Well, I didn't actually *hear* from God, but a friend of mine had a microphone with a pop-screen and a really cool computer program that edited audio recordings. He wanted to test out his equipment, and he knew I played and sang. He saw this as a chance to try out his new toys, but I saw it—like many wannabes see YouTube—as God's first open door to a professional music career. One afternoon we recorded several songs, and a few days later, he gave me a CD of my own music. I was pretty excited. Okay, that's an understatement. I was stoked!

A little while later, I found out that my college would allow me to minor in music without changing my concentration in business. I know it sounds weird—a major in business with a minor in music—but I saw this opportunity as God's second open door.

My minor in music, however, didn't start out as I thought it would. My college piano professor expected me to practice scales. But I didn't want to practice scales. I wanted to be creative. To write music. To take my emotions and feelings and put them on paper in a way that moved audiences to tears. So I dropped the class. Obviously, the professor didn't know she was working with a budding star. Maybe I should have told her.

Now, you may think that in dropping the class I would have also questioned this step as a part of God's call, but I didn't. I had already tallied this step as a confirmation of God's call, and as far as I was concerned, once something is tallied it can't be undone.

Soon after I dropped the piano class, I discovered that a famous Christian band was coming to town. Even better, a good friend of mine had been asked to take care of the band as kind of a greenroom bouncer while they were at the venue. Better still, he asked me if I wanted to hang out with the band.

Boom! There it was! God's third open door to my professional music career!

By then, I had been holding onto my CD of recorded music for a year or so, and it was burning a hole in my backpack. All of a sudden, my entire music experience came into focus, and my understanding of God's calling for my life was as clear as crystal. I didn't tell my friend what I was up to, but I did accept the invitation to hang out with the band.

A few weeks later, the Christian band came to town for the concert, and I was nervous. I also didn't feel very good about what I was getting ready to do. But I regarded my lack of peace as spiritual warfare, and I waited all night for an opportunity to give my CD to the band. After all, God had called me to become a professional musician, and this was my chance.

After the concert, it was obvious to me that the guys in the band were tired. As they started to pack up the greenroom and disassemble the stage, I knew I was running out of time to follow through on "God's opportunity." The band's lead vocalist walked off the stage to a separate room, and I followed. Kind of like a stalker—a God-stalker.

"Excuse me, sir?" I said timidly (my voice may have cracked a little bit).

"Hey, Daniel, did you enjoy the show?" the singer asked with a smile.

"Yes, it was great," I said, reveling in the fact that he remembered my name. "Do you have a moment?"

"I mean, we're in the middle of packing up, but sure, I can take a moment."

"Hey, so, I have a CD, and I feel like God is telling me to give it to you," I said. "God has given me a few songs that my mom and my friends have told me are pretty good, and I thought maybe you could put them on your next CD."

Or, better yet, maybe I could, like, join the tour? Where are we headed next?

Okay, I didn't actually ask to join the tour, but I did tell him I thought I was supposed to give him the CD. Can you imagine the awkwardness of that moment? Maybe you can. Maybe you've talked with a Christian "celebrity" about how God wants you to write a book, record a CD, or do something similar. Lucky for me, the lead singer was super compassionate and kind to me. He didn't laugh at me but accepted the CD and thanked me for it. And then he went back on stage to finish packing up.

Surprisingly, the band never called me and never asked me to join the tour. I'm not sure what happened. I'm sure it had nothing to do with my non-universal lyrics, random bad notes, and a recording that sounded like it was made in my basement (which it was). I'm sure they just lost the CD in the shuffle of packing up their gear.

The point of this story is that I was so desperate to be called by God that I convinced myself He had called me to do something He hadn't called me to do. Looking back, I'm 100 percent convinced I put words in God's mouth.

When we get to the point of believing that the only way to live a *legitimate* Christian life is by discovering and following a specialized call from God, we will search hard for God's specific will for our lives. When we can't find it—when the hide-and-seek game doesn't go the way we expect—we either give up or become so desperate for God's direction that we "hear" God calling us to do things He hasn't called us to do. Feeling the pressure to figure out what God has called us to do, we then link together coincidences and life experiences as though they are related and misinterpret them as a calling. If we do a good enough job of linking our experiences together—like I did with my meeting the famous Christian band and my made-up calling to become a rock star—we can end up creating a "calling" from nothing.

When we feel pressure to be "called," we think we have to figure it out one way or another.

In many ways, it's like we're trying to play a real-life version of "Where's Waldo," while searching for "Pokémon," while in the middle of a worldwide game of hide-and-seek. And, of course, when we try to play all three games at once, we won't win at any of them.

The blurring together of dream jobs and the calling of God is not working, and we feel even more desperate to find our answer. I believe that in order to figure this thing out, we need to figure out how to separate our searches for a dream job from God's call—to separate the games.

I don't know about you, but I'm beginning to wonder if dream jobs and the call of God are related at all. I'm concerned that the search for a dream job is something Christians have adopted from the world. I don't know this for sure, but I'm starting to wonder.

I wonder about this because of stories like that of Moses. We will look more closely at his story later on in this book, but let me quickly mention something I've noticed about the biblical story of Moses's life: God *called* Moses to lead the people of Israel, but I think we can all agree that this call was *not* Moses's dream job. In fact, Moses did everything he could to get out of following God's direction. Like a stubborn five-year-old, Moses answered God with an extensive list of excuses as to why he couldn't do what God was calling him to do.

Clearly, God called Moses to do something he didn't *want* to do. Yet we are being taught that the God who called Moses is the same God who now calls us to do whatever it takes to discover the job of our dreams. I think we need to be careful here.

Just as Moses's story jumped out to me as it regards God's call, so did Jonah's unique and specialized call from God become a reason for me to pause and wonder. When we consider Jonah's story, which we will also do more deeply later on, we can easily conclude that his calling was *not* an invitation to his dream job.

Again, I'm not saying conclusively that blurring dream jobs

and the call of God is wrong just because of the stories of two Old Testament men. But I am suggesting we need to carefully consider Moses, Jonah, and a few others before we assume that God's calling and our dream jobs are going to align into the perfect—and satisfying—life we expect. These stories should cause us to bring into question what Christian culture has taught us.

Think about it this way: If it turns out that what we consider our dream job is not at all related to God's call for our lives, yet we still try to blend the two searches into one, we will struggle to discover both.

So we need to figure this out by starting with what we know. Would you agree with that premise? I've already told you in this book that there have been several times in my life when I wasn't 100 percent sure of something. But the foundation of this book is built on a premise I believe to be absolutely true: God's calling is important, and the most reliable examples of His callings are found in the Bible.

So with that in mind—the goal of discovering what insights the Bible has about the call of God—let's see what we can find. I'm hoping you will agree with me about something I've been noticing—God has already told us a lot about what He expects from us. I hope you will find the concepts in the next few chapters to be as freeing as I've found them to be.

CHAPTER THREE

God Is Already Directing You

A man's heart plans his way,
but the LORD directs his steps.
—PROVERBS 16:9 NKJV

It was raining.

Of course it was raining. Sara lived in Oregon, near the coast, and it was always raining—at least that's how she felt. Lately, however, the daily drizzle that was once so annoying seemed to suit the state of her emotions. She was a senior in high school and just weeks away from graduation. Two different universities had already accepted her, but she couldn't decide which one to attend. The schools were nothing alike, which meant it was nearly impossible for her to consider the pros and cons of each. If they had been similar, she could have analyzed each school and made a decision to attend whichever stood out as the better option. But they weren't the same at all.

One of Sara's options—the college her dad wanted her to attend—was known for its law program. Sara didn't really want to study law, but her dad was insistent. He wanted her to be successful and to follow in the family law business. Nearly every person in Sara's family had become a lawyer. Beyond his desire for her to become a lawyer, Sara's dad also wanted her to attend the college everyone in their family had attended. It was a good school—a top-tier university, in fact—and Sara's dad told her over and over again how thankful she should be for the opportunity to attend a college most people only wish they could attend.

Sara's other option—the one she was passionately excited about—was to study photography and graphic design at a local technical college. She had always loved photography and design. Over the previous few years, she had spent her summers traveling around Oregon, capturing the diverse beauty of various landscapes. In her mind, there was nothing like the beauty of Oregon, and it made her feel alive to capture that beauty through the lens of a camera. Her favorite photos— the ones she was most proud of—were close-up shots of the moss-covered trees in a nearby national forest.

Sara tried to explain her struggle to her father many times, but he wouldn't listen.

"Dad, I want to make you happy. I want to please you and please the family. But I don't think I'm cut out to be a lawyer," Sara would explain.

"What do you mean 'not cut out to be a lawyer'?" her dad retorted. "You have excellent grades. You've been accepted into one of the top pre-law programs in the county, and your family has studied law for generations. If anyone is 'cut out' to be a lawyer, it's you."

"But I don't really want to study law. I want to take pictures—to capture moments and scenes most people miss.

You've seen what I can do. These are good photographs, and if I studied more I could—"

"Sara," her dad interrupted in a moment of frustration, "these photos are pretty, but anyone with a smartphone can capture pictures of trees. That's not a job; it's a cheap hobby that will leave you without a paycheck and sleeping on my couch."

Sara stopped talking, and tears filled her eyes. She didn't make another sound but simply left the room. Her dad was also quiet. He knew he had gone too far, but he felt like he needed to make it clear to her that her aspirations were silly. In his mind, photography just wasn't a viable career option for his daughter.

As you read Sara's story, what did you think of her dad? Do you think he was a good father or a bad father?

The answer to that question is tricky because our interpretation of the story depends on our experiences. I think all of us can agree that her dad's final comment went too far. Even if it could be argued that Sara's dad was looking out for her best interests, he went about it the wrong way. He attacked her skill, belittled her ability and passions, and demoralized her.

But there's another side to the story. Sara's dad wanted what was best for his daughter, and he knew how difficult it would be for her to build a successful career in an oversaturated market. Ask any photographer who has made it—who has built a successful business. He or she will tell you that it is really difficult to stand out because there are so many people who claim to be professional photographers. On the other hand, if Sara followed in the footsteps of her dad and the rest of her family, she would have had a guaranteed well-paying job after college. So even though Sara's dad spoke a little rudely to her, he really was trying to look out for her the best he knew how.

So I ask again, was Sara's dad a good father or a bad father? The answer is not quite as simple as we might want to think.

UNDERSTANDING THE GOODNESS OF GOD

Have you ever heard this story before? Maybe not this exact story, but something similar. Maybe in a story you've watched on TV or in a movie, the dad wanted his child to be a doctor instead of a lawyer. I'm not sure who decided that becoming a lawyer or doctor was a bad thing, but at some point a director in Hollywood felt those two occupations were in stark contrast to the dreams of young people. Maybe the director's parents wanted him to become a lawyer, but he wanted to "make movies" instead. I have to admit—the contrast between a dad's desire and a child's desire is a powerful way to express the struggle to find one's place in the world.

Sadly, many Christians see God the Father through a similar lens. We've bought into the stereotypical thinking that tells us that being obedient to God's will means we'll have to give up what we love and move to _____ (fill in the blank). Did you think of Africa or India?

But is this really who God is? Does this really express what God wants for our lives? I don't think so. I think the Bible shows us a different God than the one many of us expect.

One of the most repeated names for God in the Bible is "Father." But the Bible doesn't describe Him as any ol' father, but specifically as a *good* Father. Consider the following example:

> Don't bargain with God. Be direct. Ask for what you need. This isn't a cat-and-mouse, hide-and-seek game we're in. If your child asks for bread, do you trick him with sawdust? If he asks for fish, do you scare him with a live snake on his plate? As bad as you are, you wouldn't think of such a thing. You're at least decent to your own children. *So don't you think the God who conceived you in love will be even better?* (MATTHEW 7:7–11 MSG, italics added)

I italicized the last line of this passage because I think it suggests that God is a *good* father.

Jesus does something very powerful in this passage. He contrasts a human father's desire for what's best for his child with God the Father's desire for what's best for all His children. Most of the dads listening to Jesus that day were probably decent fathers. Like Sara's dad, they wanted what was best for their sons or daughters. Unfortunately, also like Sara's dad, their understanding of how to provide for their kids was influenced by a broken and sinful nature. Eugene Peterson paraphrased it this way, "As bad as you are," but some translations of this same passage call human fathers "evil." For example, in the New King James Version, verse 11 reads like this:

> "If you [earthly fathers], then, *being evil,* know how to give good gifts to your children, how much more will your Father who is in heaven give good things to those who ask Him!"[1]

I'm not a fan of being called "evil," but I do know I am by no means a perfect dad. I've incorrectly disciplined my kids. I've misunderstood a situation and put the wrong kid in timeout. I've had to apologize to my kids for raising my voice. I've been unreasonable, and I have expected more than I should from a seven-, five-, and three-year-old.

I think Jesus knew there were dads in His audience who, like me, had made mistakes. I also think He knew that everyone listening to Him that day could think of moments when his or her own father made a mistake. And then there were probably men and women in the audience who knew exactly what it meant to have an "evil" father. Maybe some of their dads were drunks who neglected them, and maybe others had fathers who were emotionally and physically abusive. Yet even in all of their imperfections, many of those people who had evil dads still received food.

No matter where you fit in with the examples above, I think we can all agree that even the best human daddies are imperfect, yet almost all dads—even those broken and "evil" fathers—know better than to give their kids sawdust to eat.

In contrast to human daddies who are imperfect, Jesus proclaims that God—a God who lives in heaven and who is perfect in every way—is a Father who gives even better gifts. If you can think about all of the ways in which your dad fell short, you can know that God the Father doesn't fall short in any of them. If you can think of all the ways in which your dad messed up as a parent, you can be confident that God the Father doesn't mess up in any of those ways. More than that, if you can think of all the good gifts your imperfect daddy gave you, you can be sure that your good and perfect Father in heaven will give you better gifts than you could ask or imagine (see Ephesians 3:20). In other words, even though the best of dads get it wrong sometimes, God is the perfect Dad who gets it right 100 percent of the time.

ASKING AND RECEIVING

Interestingly—and in a very applicable way to our discussion—the context of the above passage is Jesus describing the process of seeking and asking God for help. Did you notice the first line of Matthew 7:7–11? "Don't bargain with God. Be direct. Ask for what you need," Jesus said.

I'm guessing that the people Jesus talked to that day wanted help from God, and from first glance it seems that Jesus was telling them that they needed only to ask. Evidently, if we need help from God, we need only ask Him for help, and our good Father in heaven will take care of it.

Can I be transparent with you? I haven't always found this promise to be true—at least in the way I've understood it in the past. I've already spent a couple of chapters describing how God was silent when I went to Him looking for answers. In chapter 2, I described a high-stakes game of hide-and-seek—God hiding His call for my life and me trying to seek it out. Yet even after months and years of praying for God to reveal His calling and will to me, I still searched for both. So where did I go wrong?

According to Eugene Peterson—a guy who is far more knowledgeable than I am—God doesn't play "cat-and-mouse" or "hide-and-seek" games. Yet that is exactly the way in which I describe my search for God's calling. So where did I go wrong? What have I missed? If God is a good father who gives good gifts, why is He withholding the good gift of His will from me—His child?

Renowned Bible scholar Bruce Waltke puts the question this way:

> If we accept the fact that our heavenly Father loves us, and that we are His children, does it make sense that He would hide His will from us? . . . When I hear Christians talking about the will of God, they often use phrases such as "If only I could find God's will," as though He is keeping it hidden from them, or "I'm praying that I'll discover His will for my life," because they apparently believe the Lord doesn't want them to find it, or that He wants to make it as hard as possible for them to find so that they will prove their worth.... So does it make sense that He would play some sort of game with His children, hiding His will? Is it logical that the God who says He has a plan for each life would conceal that plan so that His work cannot go forward through His people?[2]

Dr. Waltke is suggesting that if we really believe that God is a good Father, we can't also believe He will play games with us and hide His will from those He loves. Those ideas are in contrast and incompatible. If God is a loving Father, He will eagerly share with us what He has planned for our lives.

Regardless of what kind of dad you had, you have some understanding—even if it's not complete—of what a good father looks like. A good father provides for his kids. A good father wants what's best for his children, and he tries to help them get there. A good father is loving and helpful, and he provides direction.

At the same time, I think we can also agree that a good father does not always tell his kids exactly what they should do but sometimes allows them to figure it out on their own. Like a good mentor, a good father asks good questions and helps his children figure out what they are supposed to do. Even if the father guides the conversation by asking the right questions and pointing the child in the right direction, he doesn't always tell his son or daughter, "This is exactly what you should do."

Yet a good father is quick to explain to his kids his expectations for how they should live their lives, especially in regard to their character and integrity.

My dad spent much of my childhood teaching me expectations. He wanted me to become a man who honored women, served others, worked hard, did well in school, reflected good character, and showed integrity. When I did the opposite of any of these expectations—such as dishonoring my mother—he used discipline to mold and shape my will. My dad was very vocal and clear about what he expected for my life.

Yet every time I asked my dad what job I should take or what career path I should choose, he was slow to help me figure out those things. My dad did not want to tell me what I should do, what I should major in, or whether I should join the family business. Instead, he looked for opportunities to shape and mold my search so I could discover what was in my best interests. He did that without neglecting all of the expectations he had already built into my character. In other words, my dad—a good father—was quick to answer questions about character and slow to answer specific questions about specific jobs.

My mentor was the same way. When I was going through the deep struggle of trying to figure out what to do with my life, my mentor never told me what he thought I should do. Instead, he asked good questions, gave me a few books to read, and pointed me toward some helpful podcasts. He also spent a lot of time with me. In the same way I have gotten frustrated with God for not giving me explicit answers, I got frustrated with my mentor for not helping me choose a specific career path. Yet, looking back, I can now see that both my dad and my mentor were extremely wise *and* good.

What if God is similar to my father and my mentor in the way He deals with questions about His will and what we are supposed to do with our lives? What if God is more concerned about our character and shaping us into the likeness of His Son than He is in making sure we do the exact job He would have for us to do? What if God—as a *good* Father—doesn't tell His kids exactly what they should do but instead focuses on the development of their integrity and character?

There's a song my son and I love to sing called "Good, Good Father." The song describes God as a good Father who loves us. I believe that! I believe that God is a good Father, even a perfect Father. And lately I've been wondering: What if this concept is the foundation for God's direction for our lives?

It makes sense to me that in the same way my dad taught me his expectations of what it means to be a man of character and integrity and to succeed in life, God—who is a far better Father than my imperfect earthly dad—has taught me His expectations. My dad—an imperfect father—told me that his will for my life was for me to become a man of integrity and character regardless of my career field.

I wonder if God—a perfect and good Father—has a similar message and will for my life?

CHAPTER FOUR

Commonly Called

This is God's will for you ...
—1 THESSALONIANS 5:18

If you don't know what to do, Google it. At least that's what I've been told. Even though it's nearly impossible to tell which content is trustworthy and which is based entirely on someone's uneducated opinion, most people still think Google can help you get going in the right direction.

If you've made it this far into the book, you have already read about my struggle to figure out God's will for my life. I never imagined I would be thirty years old and still trying to figure out who I wanted to be when I grew up. I thought for sure that by this point I would be settled into the life I dreamed about as a kid. Instead, I've worked several different jobs, not made much money, and still have yet to find a dream job.

For much of my life I've struggled to discover my unique calling, which I imagined would also be my "dream job." I've searched the Scriptures and the skies for a direct message from God, but none appeared. I did see a cloud shaped like a bunny one time, but bunny farming isn't very practical—and I'm allergic anyway—so I decided that probably wasn't God's direction.

So I continued to search and pray, and pray and search, but the only thing I discovered was frustration.

So I Googled it. Seriously. I Googled "What is God's will for my life?" I didn't find most of the links to be helpful. Many of them further blurred and confused the lines between God's calling and the search for a dream job. But after several hours of mind-numbing research, I stumbled across a list of Bible verses related to God's will.

I almost didn't click on the link. I grew up in a church that emphasized searching the Bible for God's call. Yet every time I searched the Bible for my dream job, no answers appeared. There were times when I thought the Bible offered an answer—like in college, when I thought I should join a children's ministry in South Florida. I remember praying about it and then opening the Bible and pointing haphazardly to a chapter. That chapter happened to be Matthew 19, and I read verse 14: "Let the little children come to me, and do not hinder them." Done deal! I'm supposed to have the children come unto me—or was that about Jesus?

That same "prayer plus haphazard pointing at a random verse" approach also led me to believe that Jesus didn't like it when people fell asleep during movies. Don't believe me? I didn't say it; it's right there in Scripture. "Then [Jesus] came to the disciples and found them sleeping, and said to Peter, 'What! Could you not watch with Me one hour?'" (Matthew 26:40 NKJV). I'm not sure what they were watching because I didn't read the rest of the chapter, but it's obvious the disciples—like my sister-in-law does—fell asleep after only a few minutes. I wonder if the disciples also rented the same movies at a later date because they didn't remember watching them, and then fell asleep again only to miss the movie for a second and third time?

Okay. I never actually thought Jesus was referring to watching TV or a movie in Matthew 26, but this is a great example of why Bible verses—by themselves—can mislead us when they're separated from their context.

So when I found a list of verses on "God's will," I was skeptical that they could help me figure out God's calling for my life. I had already tried the Bible route, and it seemed rather quiet on my specific role in God's story for the world. The Scriptures were full of promises about God having a plan but were quiet on the subject of God's plan *for me*.

I clicked on the link and nearly stopped reading after the first verse. Guess what they put at the top of the list? It was Jeremiah 29:11. *Really?* I thought. *I'm searching for God's specific will for my life, and you're going to offer me a general promise that says God has a plan? I've heard that my entire life! My church created a class around the topic that God has a specific plan for me—one that will lead to hope and a future. But what good is a hope and a future if I can't find out what God wants me to do?*

My skepticism at the Bible's ability to solve my dilemma grew, as did my skepticism of the website. I decided to give the list one more chance. After all, what other options did I have? It was well after midnight, and I was quickly approaching the point when I would once again give up on God's will and try again another day.

I read the second verse in the list, which began: ". . . *this is God's will for you* in Christ Jesus." Wait a second! That's the exact phrase I've been waiting to find. I've been waiting for

God to tell me, "Daniel, this is My will for you." I had been searching for God's will for as long as I could remember, and here, on the computer screen in front of me, was a verse offering God's will for *my* life. I kept reading. Actually, I decided to go back and read the entire letter of 1 Thessalonians.

The first three chapters didn't mention anything about God's specific will for me, and I nearly gave up again. The excitement of thinking I had discovered God's will had faded, and I started to think it was just a random verse taken out of context. Then I read 1 Thessalonians 4, beginning in verse 3:

> For this is the *will of God*, *your* sanctification: that you abstain from sexual immorality; that each one of you know how to control his own body in holiness and honor, not in the passion of lust like the Gentiles who do not know God; that no one transgress and wrong his brother in this matter, because the Lord is an avenger in all these things, as we told you beforehand and solemnly warned you. For God has not called us for impurity, but in holiness. Therefore whoever disregards this, disregards not man but God, who gives his Holy Spirit to you. (1 THESSALONIANS 4:3–8 ESV, italics added)

Not only did 1 Thessalonians 4:3 mention the will of God, but it also mentioned *God's very specific will for me*—to be sanctified through the work of the Holy Spirit (v. 7).

On that night when I discovered these verses about God's will, my perspective on the call of God began to shift. In the unique and slightly Russian accent of Gru from *Despicable Me*: "Light bulb." It was a "light bulb" moment, and I couldn't believe what I was reading.

Has that ever happened to you when you read Scripture? Have you ever been surprised to find something you had never noticed before in a passage you had read many times? Maybe you have read passages on God's will many times, and you don't find this section of the book to be anything new. That's okay! Or maybe you're reading these verses in 1 Thessalonians—verses you've read a thousand times—and you're having the same "aha!" moment I did. How cool is that!

As a result of my new discovery, I began to wonder: Was God concerned with telling me my career path and a specific dream job—or was He was more concerned with something else? Was He more concerned with challenging me about my character and the way I lived my life than He was about what I did for a living? Could it be that God—the good, good Father—had done exactly what I would expect from a good human father? What if He was telling me what He expects from me? What if He was saying that regardless of what career field I'm in, He desires for me to become a man of character?

My experience with Paul's first letter to the church in Thessalonica began to transform my search for God's calling. As far as I could tell, the letter had nothing to do with a particular job. Instead, the verses described the type of character God expected from those who believe in Him and follow Him. In 1 Thessalonians 5, we are told ...

- to show respect to pastors and our spiritual fathers, and esteem them highly (v. 13).
- to be at peace with everyone (v. 13).
- to comfort the fainthearted, uphold the weak, be patient with all (v. 14).

- to guard against those who would repay evil for evil, and to pursue what is in the best interests of everyone (v. 15);
- to rejoice always (v. 16);
- to pray without ceasing (v. 17);
- to always give thanks regardless of the circumstances (v. 18).

This serendipitous discovery from 1 Thessalonians inspired me to search the Bible for other verses about God's will. I discovered 1 Thessalonians 5:16–18: "Rejoice always, pray without ceasing, give thanks in all circumstances; for this is the will of God in Christ Jesus for you" (ESV). Once again, Paul mentions the "will of God." Instead of a specific call to a specific job, Paul wrote that God's will for me includes rejoicing, praying, and giving thanks regardless of the circumstances. Evidently, God has called me to a life characterized by joy, prayer, and thankfulness.

I found 1 Peter 2:15, which says, "For this is *the will of God*, that by doing good you should put to silence the ignorance of foolish people" (ESV, italics added). Wow! There was that phrase again—*the will of God*. Here was another very specific verse about God's will for my life, and it didn't apply to a specific occupation or career path. Instead, God was calling me to "do good," which is defined throughout the chapter: To be honorable (v. 12); to respect and submit to governing authority (vv. 13–14); to live as people who are free to serve God (v. 16); to honor everyone, love the brotherhood, and fear God (v. 17).

I also noticed that 1 Peter 2:15 appears in the same passage as a famous verse I had to memorize as a kid—"Live such good lives among the pagans that, though they accuse you of doing wrong, they may see your good deeds and glorify God on the day he visits us" (v. 12). This means that when I live out my calling to "do good," I will also lead people closer to God. Instead of having to become a missionary or a pastor, we can lead unbelievers to the gospel by obeying the Lord and walking with Him.

I kept searching for more Scriptures about God's calling, and I found this gem:

> Look carefully then how you walk, not as unwise but as wise, making the best use of the time, because the days are evil. Therefore do not be foolish, *but understand what the will of the Lord is.* And do not get drunk with wine, for that is debauchery, but be filled with the Spirit, addressing one another in psalms and hymns and spiritual songs, singing and making melody to the Lord with your heart, giving thanks always and for everything to God the Father in the name of our Lord Jesus Christ, submitting to one another out of reverence for Christ. (EPHESIANS 5:15–21 ESV, italics added)

Again, here was a passage of Scripture that explicitly details God's will for all believers. And again, the passage had nothing to do with a specific job or occupation. I realized that God's will for my life was not for me to become an Air Force pilot or a professional musician. God's will was for me to be wise. God's calling was for me to stay away from foolishness, including getting drunk. God's will for me was that I encourage others with songs about who God is and what He has done for me. (How cool is that? God's will is for me to sing!) God's explicit and detailed calling on my life was for me to be full of gratitude for everything He has done for me and to honor and respect others in the name of Jesus. Wow! God had a will for my life, and it was turning out to be nothing I expected.

I decided to expand my search for God's calling and consider other phrases that indicate His will for my life.

I read Micah 6:8. "He has told you, O man, what is good; and *what does the* LORD *require of you* but to do justice, and to love kindness, and to walk humbly with your God?" (ESV, italics added). The verse didn't read "this is God's will," but it seemed close enough—here is what God required of me (a.k.a. His will for my life). This verse also lacked in any instruction about a particular job I was to pursue. Instead, it told me that God planned for me to seek justice for everyone, to be characterized by kindness, and to walk with God in a spirit of respect and humility.

"CALLINGS" FROM A DIFFERENT PERSPECTIVE

As I thought about the things God was teaching me about His will for my life, I started to wonder how I had missed all these truths before. I had searched for God's will and calling for so long, and it was right in front of me the entire time. How did I not see it? Could I have been so focused on discovering God's *specific* call to a particular job that I had missed the many *common* callings from the Bible? I started to wonder: *Could God have had a specific call for my life, but this specific call had nothing to do with an occupation?*

I decided I needed to do more research.

At the time, I didn't know what to call these "callings," so I described them as *common* callings. I used the word *common* because it seemed to me that they applied to everyone who calls himself or herself a Christian. They are very specific instructions regarding how we should live our lives, and they also seemed universal for all believers in all places, in all times, and in all walks of life. For example: don't you think Micah 6:8 applies just as much to us today as it did to ancient Israel? Shouldn't we also seek justice, love mercy, and walk humbly with God? To me, this is what makes the instructions in Micah 6:8 a *common* calling.

At the same time, from a cultural perspective these specific directions are far from "common." In fact, they are decidedly uncommon. But God calls Christians to be holy, to respect authority, to be humble—not exactly the ethical standards we find in our modern culture.

Over the next few chapters we will explore many of these "common callings," and I think you will agree with me that God's instructions stand in stark contrast to the moral standards of our culture. Also, you may find these common callings to be quite convicting. I know I have! Through my journey of finding God's calling, I've discovered that His instructions often stand in stark contrast to the way I've been living my life.

PART 2

WHAT TO DO
WHEN YOU DON'T KNOW
WHAT TO DO

The Greatest Common Calling

"You can't lick the window!"
—ME

Like cliques of gossiping girls, two groups of men who would normally be in conflict with one another set aside their differences, joined together, and planned a verbal assault against someone they both viewed as a threat. The more the two groups discussed their issues with this particular individual, the more riled up they became. Although they didn't know it yet, soon—like a protest gone bad—their anger and frustration would lead them to do something terrible, something they never thought they would do. But that wouldn't happen until a few weeks after the event in question.

It was a hot day, and a thin haze of dust hung in the air. The wind had stirred up the dry, sandy soil, and most of the people in the crowd had a layer of dust caked to the sweat on their foreheads. The heat and the dust had served as a great equalizer, and the dust covered the normal signs of wealth and class. The crowd was full of men and women from all economic stations and circles of influence, yet it was nearly impossible to tell who in the crowd was rich and powerful and who was poor and lowly.

Even in the midst of a hot and dusty day, however, two groups of men still managed to distinguish themselves from the rest. These were men of influence and prestige—the leading religious scholars of the day. They were brilliant thinkers, and they spent much of their time debating answers to questions regular people didn't know to ask. Both groups wore robes, and if this story had taken place in modern times and you walked past them, you would have thought you were passing an elite graduation ceremony for an Ivy League university. They were dressed to impress in their robes and hats, and they used their clothing and positioning to let everyone in the crowd know how great they were.

Normally, the air would be full of loud arguing as the two groups met in public to disagree on deep, philosophically based religious issues. They liked to have the crowds watch them argue, because it was another opportunity to further distinguish themselves as men of brilliance. Specifically, the two groups of men enjoyed bringing up unanswerable questions so they could watch the opposing scholars squirm to provide an intelligible answer. More than that, the two groups loved to think of questions that put the opposing side into an impossible situation. It was like a game to them—to see if they could create a question about which any answer would be wrong to at least one person in the audience.

You could say both groups of scholars enjoyed stirring up the crowds to respond negatively to one another, and they enjoyed watching the opposing group try to backpedal out of nearly causing a riot. Over time, it became clear that, like the

Republicans and Democrats of today, these two groups would never be able to get along again. So you can imagine everyone's surprise when the two groups stood together and aimed their divisive questions and word traps toward an outsider—someone who didn't belong to either prestigious group.

Over the previous few years, the two groups had watched as a small-town teacher rose in popularity and influence. At first, the scholars listened in jealous appreciation of the wisdom of the no-name rabbi. In fact, some of the scholars had been around twenty or so years earlier, when this man—who was then a young boy—sat in the synagogue and reasoned with them at a level well beyond His years. At that time, they were so impressed with Him that they thought for sure He would grow up to become one of them—to one day share a seat of influence. The young man never had a chance to pursue scholarship, however. Instead, His father apprenticed Him to be a stonemason and woodworker.

Years later, the religious scholars were amazed to see this young carpenter and stonemason—now an adult—travel the countryside with an entourage of disciples and fans. They appreciated a lot of what He taught, and they had enjoyed a few sermons He had preached. One sermon in particular, a sermon about not being anxious because God will provide, had been especially pleasing to them. In that same sermon, this man had shown His aptitude for applying the Law in a manner similar to the religious scholars. He took their laws and expounded upon them to make them more understandable. For example, He taught that murder is more than just killing someone. He said that someone is also guilty of murder if he simply thought hate-filled thoughts toward another person. It was a convicting teaching, and though neither group of scholars necessarily agreed nor disagreed, they were still impressed with the logic and debate skill the no-name teacher demonstrated.

Unfortunately for them, however, the man slowly became too influential, and soon He threatened the influence and power of the two groups of religious scholars. More than that, there were a few instances in which this guy had presented His audience with statements that flirted with flat-out blasphemy. It soon became clear that the scholars needed to come together to discredit Him and remind the crowd that He was still an uneducated small-town simpleton who really didn't know what He was talking about.

They thought it would be easy. After a quick meeting, the group came up with a question they knew would trip Him up. In fact, the groups of scholars didn't even come to the show-down. Instead, they sent their representatives to trap Jesus in an unanswerable question: "Teacher," the scholarly disciples would ask Jesus, "should we pay taxes?"

Like today, most of the people at that time had strong opinions about taxes. Many thought they should keep the money and not give Rome any coin of any size. Many others—like the Roman soldiers who often listened to Jesus—thought taxes were necessary for various reasons, including their own pay-checks. It was one of those questions that trapped everyone. Jesus couldn't answer it without making half of the crowd very angry.

Although the scholars didn't go to hear Jesus's response, they still waited to hear the good news. They expected their disciples to come back and tell them how Jesus had been arrested for siding with the Israelites and inciting a political riot. But they didn't. Instead, with sullen faces showing obvious embarrassment, their disciples came back to explain how Jesus had wiggled out of it. As they explained Jesus's response, the scholars sat back in frustrated appreciation at His wisdom. For a moment, they even marveled at His response.

Realizing it was going to take more than a simple question to discredit the small-town teacher, the two groups of scholars split up into their prospective teams and started thinking of new questions to ask—questions intended to trap Jesus in a web of logic from which He couldn't escape. The Sadducees were the first group of scholars to think of a good riddle, and this time, instead of trusting a disciple to communicate the question, they decided to travel to the center of town themselves and ask Jesus their "unanswerable question."

"Teacher," the Sadducees asked in a respectful tone, "Moses—the forefather of our law and the greatest leader in the history of our nation—taught us that if a man dies without children, that out of respect for the dead his brother should marry the widow and create an heir for the deceased. What if there were seven brothers, and each brother kept dying? The widow would end up marrying all seven of them. When she ended up in heaven, to whom would she be married?" (see Luke 20:27–40). Ironically, the Sadducees didn't even believe in the resurrection of the dead (see Acts 23:8).

As before, the Pharisees waited for the Sadducees to come back and tell of their victory. The Sadducees came back defeated, however—and embarrassed. The Pharisees should have known the Sadducees couldn't do it, and they said as much. "Don't send a child to do a man's job," one of the Pharisees whispered. After all, the two groups argued over these issues because they despised one another. The Pharisees should have known the Sadducees couldn't pull off tricking Jesus. So they decided to take care of the matter themselves.

The Pharisees picked the man from their group, the debate champion who had distinguished himself in arguments with the Sadducees. He was a lawyer and had made his living by trapping people in webs of questioning. He was a master at asking impossible questions and watching the accused—whether guilty or innocent—fade under the weight of accusation and guilt. The Pharisees knew this lawyer could trap Jesus, and the lawyer knew it too. Even the Sadducees expected him to come back victorious, to their shame.

"Teacher," the lawyer asked in a respectful and flattering tone, "what is the greatest commandment in all of the Law? If one of the simpler minds listening to us today was only able to keep one commandment, which commandment should he focus on?" (See Matthew 22:36.)

Mic drop.

The lawyer nearly walked away, confident he had won. Israel's Law—in its entirety—was the most sacred part of their history and culture. Everyone was dedicated to following the Law, and they regarded the Law of Moses at a higher level than Americans have ever regarded the United States Constitution. The Law was the supreme code of the land, and no part of it could be separated from the rest. No commandment could be greater than any other commandment.

The lawyer was sure he had won, and he expected Jesus to walk away defeated ... and alone. Finally, the crowd would see Him for the false teacher He was, and they would realize He was inadequate and not educated enough to understand the deeper and more important aspects of Moses's Law. The lawyer looked at Jesus and smirked—the same smirk he showed defendants in the courtroom, the defendants who knew they would now be condemned because they couldn't argue with such a master of debate.

Jesus looked back at the lawyer, but without so much as a hint of condemnation or anger. In fact, the lawyer was surprised to see compassion and kindness in Jesus's eyes. But he also noticed something else: Jesus's eyes were filled with a fiery confidence—as if He had known the question ahead of time and was prepared with a passionate response. Clearly, Jesus knew what the lawyer was up to, and He knew He could answer the question. Yet He still somehow cared about the lawyer who tried to trap Him. How Jesus communicated all of this through one look, the lawyer didn't know. The closest he had come to a similar experience was the way his mom looked at him when he was in trouble—a unique combination of love and stern discipline. Although the lawyer had seen confidence in the eyes of adversaries, he had never seen compassion in the eyes of the Sadducees or one of the defendants he had arraigned. He began to feel uncomfortable as Jesus responded:

> "You shall love the Lord your God with all your heart and with all your soul and with all your mind. This is the great and first commandment. And a second is like it: You shall love your neighbor as yourself. On these two commandments depend all the Law and the Prophets." (MATTHEW 22:37–40 ESV)

I think the story above—and specifically the verses quoted at the end of that story—best summarizes the message of this book. Like a thesis-driven paper for school, the Greatest Commandment and the One Like It are the summary statements of God's expectations for our lives.

Jesus, in a moment of being questioned about the Law, summarized all of God's expectations in just a few short sentences. I think Jesus's summary may be the best possible outline for us to use for the next few chapters on specific common callings. After all, don't you think the Greatest Commandment and the One Like It both apply to us today? Don't you think you and I and all Christians are called to love God wholeheartedly and to love others?

Surely, these are the greatest of all the common callings.

Jesus's response to the Pharisees on that hot and dusty day thousands of years ago was not something He made up on the spot. It wasn't an off-the-cuff response. Jesus didn't create a new commandment to answer the question of the lawyer. He was quoting the most "fundamental of Israel's 'credal' traditions"—the cornerstone of the Law of Moses.[1]

Like the preambles to the constitutions of countries like the United States and of the Republic of Rwanda or to the *Declaration of the Rights of Man and of the Citizen* in French law, or the many other foundational statements that summarize the purpose and mission of various sovereign nations, the "Shema" was the defining statement of the Law of Moses. For the nation of Israel and the Jews, the Shema is a big deal.

According to people who know a lot more about this passage of Scripture than I do, the passage Jesus quoted—Deuteronomy 6:4-5—is called the "Shema" because that's the first word of the passage. It means, "Hear," and is "a favorite form of address in Deuteronomy."[2] According to some scholars, the "summons, Hear, O Israel … is similar to … parents calling a child's attention to their teaching for the child's own good."[3]

———◇———

Over the past several years, I've had to teach my kids things I never thought I would have to teach.

Not long ago, I decided to be a good dad and take my son out for an "adventure." I'd heard parenting experts say it's important to take your kids out for "dates," but what dad wants to take his son on a date? So instead, my sons and I call them "adventures."

On the night in question, my son and I decided to go to his favorite restaurant—a very busy restaurant known as Chick-fil-A. We lived in Colorado at the time, and it was a rather cold night during flu season. I mention flu season because my extremely protective wife wanted to make sure I didn't take my son to a place where he would catch the bug. She strongly discouraged this chicken restaurant simply because it was so busy.

She knew without a doubt that at least a handful of contagious people had eaten there on that very day, and her last comment to me as we walked out the door was, "If you insist on taking him there, please take the necessary precautions!" That statement, of course, would put me on the hook for any kind of illness our son might contract.

After ordering our food, my son and I sat down at a table. Before I let him get comfortable, I placed a protective plastic barrier between his hands and the surface of the table. He was four years old, and I knew he would end up placing at least one chicken nugget or waffle fry on the wooden petri dish known as a fast-food restaurant table. I was right. During our meal, my son placed most of his chicken nuggets and waffle fries on the plastic placemat. He also squirted his ketchup on it.

I was feeling really good about our "adventure." I had done my job as a parent and covered the table. I'm pretty sure I also used anti-bacterial hand soap to clean his hands after the meal. Because our "adventure" was going so well, I decided to let him trade in the book that came with his kid's meal for an ice cream cone.

"Fin," I asked with a smile, knowing how excited he was about to become, "would you like some ice cream?"

I got the response I was going for. His face broke out into a huge smile. He didn't say, "Yes." Instead, he made some sort of excited growl that I took for a "Yes!"

We were sitting nearly right next to the counter, so I left him at the table while I went up to trade out his children's book. I decided I too might want something, and I took my eyes off Fin for a few seconds while I ordered some ice cream.

Less than ten seconds later, I turned around—and was mortified to see my son—my sweet, sweet son—*licking the restaurant window next to our table*! I'm guessing the window was cold, and our conversation about ice cream had caused his licking reflex to become uncontrollable. I lunged back to the table and scolded him.

"Finley, what are you doing? You can't lick the window! It's covered in germs. You will get sick, buddy. Look at Daddy . . ."

Finley looked back at me with the same enthusiastic smile he had for the ice cream. Evidently, the window had tasted great.

"More than just getting sick, it's not polite to lick the windows. Big boys don't do things like that. You want people to think you are a big boy, right? So you can't lick windows. Please don't ever do that again."

"Okay, Daddy," he said. For some reason, I doubted he would remember this conversation.

Just then, our ice cream came to the table, and he began to destroy his cone.

I'm telling you, when that kid eats ice cream, he does it with enthusiasm. Evidently, he licks windows with the same vigor.

As I watched my son consume his cone, I looked back at the window and noticed a nice, long lick mark surrounded by hand prints. I didn't think all of those handprints were his.

In a similar way to my teaching Finley not to lick a restaurant window, God teaches His kids principles designed for their good. In the Shema, God asks the children of Israel—His children—to listen to His teaching. More than just giving a command to *hear*, God, like a parent, also asks His children to do something. As one person put it, "They [the Israelites] were not merely spectators at a divine 'show,' but recipients of divine revelation in words. They were to hear the truth and then respond to it."[4]

And what were they to respond to? A call to love God with all that they are—heart, soul, and might. It is the foundation for Moses's Law—the preamble—the cornerstone on which all of Israel's covenant history with God is founded.

It's no wonder the Pharisees marveled at Jesus's response—and no longer wanted to ask Him questions. Like a pastor who takes two passages of Scripture and draws between them a valid and powerful connection you and I hadn't noticed before, Jesus brought the audience back to the foundational principle of their purpose and mission as a nation and a "people."

I think this passage is important because Jesus takes what was a burden, the weight of a complicated law code, and makes it simple. As an American, I think about the Constitution and how complicated it is, especially now. There are people who spend their lives studying the intricacies of what has become an extremely complicated system of laws and amendments. In some ways, I wish someone like Jesus would come to simplify our laws down to two simple principles.

More than just simplifying the Law for the Jews and answering the unanswerable question of the prestigious lawyer, I think Jesus was also saying something to the rest of the audience—an audience that most likely consisted of some people outside the Jewish faith. I think it's reasonable to assume that God's expectations for everyone, even those of us who are not Israelites, are so much simpler than we make them out to be. Notice I didn't use the word *easier*. I used the word *simpler*. Everything you and I read in the Bible—every story, passage, and verse—is summed up in two simple commands, the greatest commands, to love God and to love others. Don't you think this is meant for us as well? Don't you think you and I are *called* to love God and love others?

Like a dad in a restaurant trying to get the attention of his son who is licking the window, God—our good Father—asks you and me to "Shema (hear)" what He has to say. And what is God saying to us? God is calling all of us to the same expectations as those He placed on the Israelites. He is calling us to love Him with all that we are and to love others as much as we love ourselves. This is the greatest common calling of all.

CHAPTER SIX

A Common Calling to Love God (Worship)

Tyger Tyger, burning bright,
In the forests of the night;
What immortal hand or eye,
Could frame they fearful symmetry?
—WILLIAM BLAKE, "The Tyger,"
Songs of Innocence and of Experience

It was late—*really* late—and I was absolutely exhausted. That morning I had awakened extra early to go to work, and I had comforted myself with the resolution that I would reward an early day's work by going to bed extra early.

That didn't happen.

My goal was to be in bed by 9 p.m. and it was now 11:30. I finally closed up the house, brushed my teeth, prayed, and then crawled—*literally* crawled—into bed. As I pulled throw pillows off my bed—the types of pillows that only show up after marriage—I was surprised to find a small person hidden in the mound of plush comfort. My little girl, who had just recently turned three years old, had sneaked into our room and into our bed.

I had wondered why she had been so quiet. Normally, Ava is the queen of not going to bed when she's supposed to. Something in her little strong will sees bedtime as a suggestion, and my wife and I had yet to train that out of her. She's the one who would go all day without acting like she's potty-trained—making mistakes because she was focused on playing—and then suddenly, at bedtime, she needs to go potty. Several times. I think she had learned that regardless of how serious my wife and I are about bedtime, we always let our kids go to the bathroom. She definitely uses that to her advantage.

Tonight, however, she hadn't come out of her room at all. She went straight to sleep! My wife and I had marveled at the potential celebratory moment that our daughter—our sweet girl with a very strong will—finally listened to us and went straight to bed. Well, she did go straight to bed, just not to *her* bed! More than that, our little girl had hidden herself in pillows so she wouldn't get caught. She's so clever!

I stared at her for a few minutes and was overcome by how thankful I am for her. I had prayed for many years that the Lord would bless us with a baby girl. I had been disappointed to find out through an ultrasound that our third child would be another boy. I love my boys so much, but I really wanted a baby girl.

When my wife and I were married, we decided we would have six kids, and we had picked the first two names we really liked. We picked "Noah" for our first boy and "Ava" for our first girl. We already had the middle names picked out as well, and originally my wife and I were going to name our girl "Ava Rayne" (pronounced *Rain*). Ava means "song," and Rayne, well, that's just a different way to spell the word *rain*. Her name was going to mean "Song of the Rain"—beautiful, tranquil, and sweet.

With every child my wife and I had, our desired number of children decreased. After two boys, we were down to wanting only one more child. And I really, really wanted a baby girl! For six years of marriage, I had prayed for the Lord to give us a girl. But the ultrasound—the almighty demystifying ultrasound—had dashed my hopes. I still knew there was a chance the ultrasound was wrong, and I still prayed for a girl ... but I also prayed that the Lord would prepare me for life with three boys. We knew we would be done having children after our third was born, and I had nearly given up hope.

Then *she* was born—my sweet Ava was born. Upon seeing her for the first time, I immediately knew we had to change her middle name. Instead of Ava Rayne, my wife and I decided to name her Ava Eliana. Eliana means "God answers" or "God has answered my prayer," and I wanted her name to reflect the fact that God had heard my prayer and blessed us in a way I hadn't expected. Ava Eliana—Song that God Answers. It was perfect.

Now that you know a little of my girl's story, I think you can see why I didn't get angry when I found her asleep in my bed. Instead, I slid in next to her and watched her sleep. I also thanked God for her. I was overcome by her beauty and tenderness. I was overwhelmed by my love for her. The only way I knew to express it was to cuddle up and praise God for His answered prayer.

I can't be sure, but after considering the research I've done for this book, I think I may have been worshipping God that night. My love for my little girl had led me to appreciate what God had done for me. Her tender beauty stirred something in my heart, something I can't quite describe. This stirring was more than just appreciation for the scientific process that had occurred as the result of the information stored in her DNA and RNA. My soul was stirred. My heart was stirred. It was as if the sleeping face of my beautiful baby girl had given me a glimpse of a beautiful God.

Beauty and *love.* Two words we often hear in reference to God, yet they are the two concepts I have the hardest time relating to Him. Maybe you find it easy to love God and find Him beautiful, but I don't. For some reason, the concepts of loving God and finding Him beautiful seem weird to me.

I think there are two reasons for this. First, I've been taught that God is a dude. I don't mean that in disrespect, but every metaphor for God I've heard, most church leaders I've met, and most Scripture passages I can think of refer to God as male. I'm aware this is not completely accurate because God transcends gender and probably doesn't have a "sex" in the way we understand it. But it's what I've been taught. So when someone tells me I should find God beautiful, that would be like someone telling me I need to find my friends Michael or Jarred beautiful, and that's not going to happen!

Second, sometimes I feel like God is too far away to love. I cognitively acknowledge that He's here with me (in this room as I write this chapter), but I don't necessarily feel that way most of the time. I think of God as a powerful entity in a place called heaven—a place I think is pretty far away—and as a quotation from N. T. Wright will point out later in this chapter, my understanding of God's "otherness" is the foundational cause of my struggle to love Him. Yet *love* is the exact word Jesus used in the Greatest Common Calling, which means I better try to figure this out.

In the previous chapter, I pointed out that Jesus said that the Greatest Commandment, which I referred to as the Greatest Common Calling, is to "love the Lord your God with all your heart and with all your soul and with all your mind" (Matthew 22:37 ESV).

It's interesting to me that the greatest command would be a command to love. Why use that word? Why not say the Greatest Commandment is to "fear" God, "stand in awe" of God, or "obey" God (three things I feel I've been taught to focus on)? Instead, the Greatest Commandment—the summary of all of God's expectations on our lives—is a call to *love* God with our entire person.

LOVE AND ITS CONNECTION TO WORSHIP

James K. A. Smith, one of the brilliant thinkers of our day, suggests that love is the defining factor of what it means to be human. According to him, "*we are what we love*, and our love is shaped, primed, and aimed by *liturgical practices* that take hold of our gut and aim our heart to certain ends."[1] Later, he makes it personal and declares, "I am what I love."[2] In other words, love is the defining factor that molds us into the men and women we currently are and will become.

I've spent a lot of time thinking about Smith's phrase "I am what I love," and I would encourage you to do the same. It's something worth meditating on. The longer I think about it, however, the more complicated I find it to be. I have found this concept to have many layers, and it wasn't until I remembered a key lesson from one of my high school teachers that it began to make sense.

"Life is all about relationships," said Mrs. Williams, who spoke fluent Spanish and French, and who was really good at teaching both languages. Not everyone who speaks a second language is also good at teaching, but Mrs. Williams was a great teacher. One of the best parts of her courses was that once a month we got to cook food in her classroom. If you took Spanish, that meant a Spanish meal once a month. If you took French, that meant you got to eat French food once a month. And if you were on student government—over which Mrs. Williams was the advisor—you got to enjoy the leftovers of both classes. I was privileged to enjoy all three. I took Spanish. I took French. And I was also on student government. I ate well in high school.

If you took one of Mrs. Williams's classes, however, you would find that her passion was not helping students speak second and third languages or to provide meals to make class time more fun and interesting. Mrs. Williams was passionate about one thing: helping people build relationships with God and with others. It didn't matter how many of her classes you took, she always began each course with the same foundational lesson plan.

First, she taught us the importance of language as the primary way in which people communicate and build relationships. It made sense to me. If you can't speak to someone, it's hard to build a relationship with that person. I think this is also why she did meals in the classroom; she wanted to give her students ample time to interact with one another.

Second, Mrs. Williams taught us that "Life is all about relationships." That was her own phrase. Every student who took her class joked around about her "famous" quote, and some of her lazier students (Ahem, me) would sometimes write in that phrase when we didn't know an answer to a question on a test or quiz. If "Jesus" or "God" is always the correct answer to a question in Sunday school, "relationships" should have always been the correct answer in Mrs. Williams's class. I write, "should have been" because I still got questions wrong. Evidently, even she didn't think "Hola Amigo!" translated into "life is all about relationships."

I think James K. A. Smith is working off the same foundation Mrs. Williams taught in all of her classes. Smith writes that humans—more than being thinkers or believers—are primarily lovers in pursuit of something to love. He suggests that God created us to love, just like Mrs. Williams taught that God created us for relationships. And I think both James Smith and Mrs. Williams would agree: our love needs an object, a destination at which to aim.

So if we were created to love and love needs a destination, then our lives will naturally become absorbed by the search for an object to love. That's what Smith means when he writes, "We are what we love." We are completely and utterly driven, obsessed, and absorbed by the pursuit of love. If this is true, than you and I have two very important questions to consider:

1. What do we love?
2. Where is love leading us?

The answers to these questions will dictate what our life is about and what we do with it.

SHAPED BY LITURGICAL PRACTICES

More than just considering what we love, Smith encourages us to also consider what shapes our love. According to him, "our love is shaped, primed, and aimed by *liturgical practices* that take hold of our gut and aim our heart to certain ends."[3] For those of us who are strangers to terms like "liturgical practices," an easier way to think of these "practices" might be through looking at the content of a children's book that helped me understand the concept more clearly. The book is titled *The Rhythm of My Day,* and my kids love it. The story describes the different parts of a child's daily experience—waking up, getting dressed, taking a bath, eating food, taking a nap, and going to bed. Each page ends with, "Rhythm, the rhythm, the rhythm of my day."[4]

We all have a rhythm to our lives—habits we act upon every day without thinking about it—and those rhythms shape us. But where do our rhythms and habits come from, and what do they communicate about who we are, what we care about, and what we seek? According to Smith, our habits begin and end with our pursuit of love and the destination at which our love is aimed. Whatever our lives are about, whatever our daily rhythms indicate to be our priorities and direction—that is what we love.

I think Smith uses the word *liturgical* because he wants people like me to realize that the pursuit of love he describes is deeper than a passion for dark chocolate peanut butter cups or strawberry cheesecake ice cream. Smith sees our pursuit of love as *the pursuit of something ultimate*—either God or something to replace God. As a result, he sees the rhythms formed by our pursuit of love as more than just daily habits like brushing our teeth or putting on pajamas before bed. The practices and rhythms we're talking about are the rhythms of worship we value the most.

In other words, whatever our lives are about—the daily rhythms that indicate our priorities and direction—is what we love and therefore also what we worship.

According to N. T. Wright, "Worship is what we were made for."[5] Smith says the purpose of our lives is to love, and Wright says the purpose of our lives is to worship. I don't think these ideas contradict each other; instead, I think both of these guys are trying to tell us something, namely, that we are what we love, that our love is shaped by our worship, and that we were made to worship. If this is true, then I think we could also say *our call to love God is a call to worship.* As Wright put it, "Worship is nothing more nor less than love on its knees before the beloved."[6] So somehow love and worship are connected, and both shape and define us.

If it is true that the call to love God is also a call to worship God, then we could modify the Greatest Common Calling (also known as the Greatest Commandment) and replace the word *love* with *worship.* If that's allowed, the new version would read, "Worship the Lord your God with all your heart and with all your soul and with all your mind."

Just as love encompasses all of life, our worship is an

all-inclusive lifestyle that defines and shapes us. David Peter-son—another pretty smart theologian—suggests that worship, "far from being a peripheral subject"—meaning something rel-atively unimportant to our day-to-day lives—"has to do with the fundamental question of how we can be in a right relation-ship with God and please Him in all that we do."[7]

Again, if I understand what these scholars are trying to communicate, then the following is true: *We are creatures of worship because we are creatures of love, and our habits—the liturgical rhythms that shape our lives—are the true indicators of our worship because they shape and confirm what we truly love.* Did you follow that? Maybe this diagram will help:

We are what we love.

What we love is also what we worship.

What we worship defines our priorities, which turns around and shapes our love.

A RICH GUY WITH A MESSED-UP LOVE

A long time ago, there was a really wealthy guy who was also known for his superb moral excellence. He was brilliant in business and very ethical. He was also a leader who was responsible for large group of followers. I don't know if he owned a big business with lots of employees, or if he was a political leader, but either way, I get the sense that all who followed him deeply respected him. Interestingly, he was also young, which says a lot about the type of character he must have displayed. It's rare to find a rich, young, and successful leader who is so well respected.

I think much of his success can be attributed to his reputation as a "checklist" guy. I'm guessing he had a checklist for leading people, a checklist for his businesses, and a checklist for morality. He probably kept the lists in a journal and updated them constantly.

The rich young leader had heard about this teacher of religion who was a brilliant thinker and who seemed to have an answer for everything. This young man felt the teacher had the answers to most aspects of his life, but he was still a little confused on what he considered to be the most important question of all. He felt he had finally found the guy who could answer him.

"Teacher, what must I do to live forever in heaven and inherit eternal life?" the rich young leader asked.

"You know the commandments," Jesus responded.

"Do not murder
 Do not commit adultery
 Do not steal
 Do not bear false witness

99

Do not defraud
Honor your father and mother."

The young leader must have felt a sense of excitement as he mentally checked off the list Jesus gave him. He loved lists, and he was thrilled that Jesus thought the same way he did. He didn't mean to smirk with confidence, but the rich young leader … well, he was just that—young. I know, because I'm young and tend to think I've got it all together too.

"Done! I've done all those things," he reported. "Seriously, I've done all of those things since I was a young boy. I haven't killed anyone, and I've been faithful to my wife. I run a good business and haven't stolen or defrauded anyone. I haven't even lied about any of my neighbors, and I always honored and obeyed my father and mother. (I wish his mom had been around to respond to this claim!) I've done all of this, Jesus! Thank you for such great news!"

"Wait a second," Jesus said, stopping the rich young leader from continuing his celebration. "There's one more thing."

"What is it? What could I possibly lack?"

Jesus looked into the rich young leader's eyes. It was obvious that Jesus cared for the young man and wanted him to inherit eternal life. Yet, as I imagine was often the case with Jesus, there was glimpse of something else in His eyes as well: a knowing—a painful knowing. Even the rich young ruler began to brace himself for what came next. He could tell Jesus was about to ask for a lot.

Jesus told him, "I want you to go and sell everything you have—including all your land and businesses—and give the money to the poor. After you do that, come follow Me and you will inherit the eternal life you seek."

It was a painful moment. For the rich young leader, it no doubt felt as if time had stopped. He was deeply affected by what Jesus had just said, and it seemed he was about to get sick to his stomach.

The young man wanted to get angry and tell Jesus that there was obviously a misunderstanding. As good as Jesus was at teaching, he may have thought, He was obviously not in touch with the real world. The rich young leader wanted to tell Jesus that He didn't get it—that He just didn't understand. But he could tell from the look in Jesus's eyes that He understood exactly what was going on inside him.

Slowly, the rich young leader turned around and walked away. He was frustrated but also conflicted. Something inside of him wanted to do exactly what Jesus requested, but he knew that giving up his home and privilege would be a stupid business decision. Also, he was responsible for the livelihoods of a lot of people who looked up to him. God wouldn't really want him to cause a small spike in unemployment, would He?

Here's the problem: The rich young leader loved his money, and that led him to worship financial position and prestige. The young man patterned his life after financial gain, which in turn led to his response to Jesus: "He went away grieving, for he was one who owned much property" (Mark 10:22 NASB).

To me, the story of the rich young ruler illustrates how love and worship are connected. More than that, the story shows us how the things we truly love can direct us away from God. The rich young ruler defined his life by his wealth, and his love for money led him away from God. He walked away from Jesus. His love was misdirected, and it cost him eternity with God.

We are what we love.

What we love is also what we worship.

What we worship is what we pattern our lives after, which in turn shapes and informs our worship.

But the story of the rich young ruler is not included in the Scriptures just so we can both judge and feel sorry for the guy with a misdirected love. I think the story is included in Scripture because all of us have the potential to love something else more than we love God. And if we love something else more than we love God, we could end up doing the same thing—walking away from Him and missing out on the abundant and full life He has for us. So the questions for us today are these:

1. What do you love?
2. In which directions are your "loves" pointing you, and in what ways are your "loves" shaping you?
3. If you follow your heart, where will you end up?

HOW DO WE WORSHIP?

Now that we've considered the connection between love and worship, I wonder if we might be able to figure out some ways in which we can worship God. I can't help but think that at this point, all we've concluded is that in order to worship God we need to make sure He's our first love. While that's certainly true, I also want to know what to do—how can I worship God today?

N. T. Wright suggests that the common understanding of worship is to tell God how great He is ... "But the word *worship* means, literally, 'worth-ship': to accord worth, true value, to something, to recognize and respect it for the true worship it has."[8] If this is true, then you and I should spend some time each day praising God simply because of who He is.

Consider the following example from Scripture:

> Ascribe to the LORD, all you families of nations, ascribe to the LORD glory and strength. Ascribe to the LORD the glory due his name; bring an offering and come into his courts. Worship the LORD in the splendor of his holiness; tremble before him, all the earth. (PSALM 96:7–9 ESV)

Yet Wright warns us, "It's not enough to think of God's greatness and majesty, his power and sovereignty, his holiness and absolute otherness."[9] Wright doesn't want us to forget God's beauty: "Our ordinary experiences of beauty are given to us to provide a clue, a starting point, a signpost, from which we move on to recognize, to glimpse, to be overwhelmed by, to adore, and so to worship, not just the majesty, but the beauty of God himself."[10]

This is where the story of my daughter comes in. It was in that moment late at night, when I discovered her in our bed, when I was able to get a glimpse of the beauty and glory of God. I was amazed by the beauty and the tenderness He exhibited in the sweet and elegant face of my baby girl. At that moment, I was able to worship God not only for who He is, but also for what He had done.

On a deeper level, our worship of God for what He has done will always lead us to Jesus. After all, God's ultimate sacrifice for us was the sentencing of His Son to death on our behalf. As a dad, I can't imagine sacrificing my son for someone else, yet God did just that for you and me. What great love God must have for us!

"If Jesus is to be the lens through which you glimpse the beauty of God," Wright suggests, "you will discover what it means to worship, because you will discover what it means to be loved."[11]

Did you catch that? Somehow, we are back to the subject of love again. Love, beauty, worship, and the sacrifice of Christ are all tied together.

If you are like me, you may be sitting back in awe at the way God weaves together concepts like love, worship, and beauty, but you still may be confused on what to *do* about it.

I think most of us struggle to worship, and there are many different reasons for that. For me, it's because I struggle to get out of my own head. This may sound weird, so allow me to explain. I struggle to understand the concept of worship beyond a mental exercise of my brain acknowledging the existence of an all-powerful God who is in heaven. In other words,

I've got the whole "tell God how great He is" thing down. I can do that. But how do I get past what Wright described as the "distant acknowledgement of majesty."[12]

Not only do I struggle to understand worship outside of a mental acknowledgement of who God is but I also struggle to comprehend what He has done. I have a dimly lit and out-of-focus idea of what the salvation offered in Christ really means—the weight it really carries—and that leads me to a dimly lit and out-of-focus idea of what worshipping God for what He's done through Christ looks like. So how do I get it in focus? I'm starting to sound like the rich young leader—asking God for a list so I can check off the steps to successful worship.

Unfortunately and fortunately—yes, it is both—God makes worship possible. According to one of the smart guys I leaned on heavily for this chapter, "Worship is something made possible for us by God."[13] Just as sanctification and the call to perfection are impossible without the Holy Spirit, the common call to worship is also impossible without God's leadership. It is God who stirs our hearts with glimpses of beauty. It is God who created a world with things that amaze us. And it is God who sent His Son to die for us and take upon himself our shame. God has done the work, which makes our job simple. We respond:

> Worship is humble and glad; worship forgets itself in remembering God; worship celebrates the truth as God's truth, not its own. True worship doesn't put on a show or make a fuss; true worship isn't forced, isn't half-hearted, doesn't keep looking at its watch, doesn't worry what the person in the next pew may be doing. True worship is

open to God, adoring God, waiting for God, trusting God even in the dark.[14]

So the common call to love God is really a call to worship, which is ultimately a call to respond to who God is and what He's done. I think I can do that. At least I can try.

CHAPTER SEVEN

A Common Calling to Love Others

For Mercy has a human heart
Pity, a human face:
And Love, the human form divine,
And Peace, the human dress.

. . .

And all must love the human form,
In heathen, Turk, or Jew.
Where Mercy, Love, and Pity dwell
There God is dwelling too.
—WILLIAM BLAKE, "The Divine Image"

Hank didn't have a choice. He had been out of work for several months, had already lost his house to foreclosure, and was struggling to provide food for his wife and kids. Every job Hank applied for had fallen through, except one. He had been offered an executive-level position with a small factory based in the middle of a violent inner-city neighborhood. If Hank took the job, he would be commuting through a bad area of town.

But it was worse. When Hank lost his previous job, he also lost both of his cars. His primary transportation was a company vehicle that had been taken away when he was laid off. His second car—a van he had purchased—was repossessed when Hank stopped making his payments. As a result, he was left with only his mountain bike—a very nice one—as a mode of transportation. That meant Hank would not only be commuting through the inner city but he would also be riding a nice mountain bike while wearing an executive style suit and tie.

Hank was afraid, and he should have been. But what other choice did he have? If he was going to take care of his family, he needed a job.

One early morning on the way to work, around 6:30, Hank was attacked. He barely saw the guy coming through the thick morning fog. By the time he saw the look of aggression in the man's face, it was too late. Hank was mugged, stripped, and left on the street with a gaping knife wound in his left side. He tried to call out for help, but just taking a deep breath so he could talk proved too painful for him.

Hank drifted in and out of consciousness. After what seemed like forever, He saw a figure coming through the fog. The man got close enough that Hank could see the cross around his neck and the Christian tracts he held in his hands. *It's going to be okay*, he thought, just as he blacked out.

What Hank didn't see because he went unconscious was that the man in the fog—a businessman and street evangelist—nearly stepped on him. When he finally saw Hank, he felt compassion for him, but realizing that he had been mugged and stabbed, he thought about how dangerous this area of the city really was. Although the Christian businessman felt guilty for not helping Hank, he left—afraid of what might happen to him if he lingered.

When Hank came back to consciousness, he quickly looked around for the man with the cross and the tracts. But he was gone. Just then, another person came into view, and this time it was obviously a religious person. The woman wore a collar, and Hank assumed she must be a priest. A scratchy and fluid-filled "Help!" was all he could muster, but it was enough to get her attention. She made eye contact with him, and he was relieved to know that someone saw him. But as Hank blacked out for a second time, the woman used his unconsciousness as an opportunity to disappear into the fog.

Hank woke up again and was confused. *I must be seeing things*, he thought. Just then, he heard a loud screeching sound and looked up to see the bumper of a yellow checkered van within inches of his head. Again, he fainted.

The taxi driver—an Iranian man—got out of his van and rushed to Hank's side. He ripped off his shirt and did the best he could to bandage the knife wound and stop the bleeding. Although he knew it wasn't the best idea to lift someone who is that badly injured, he didn't see much of a choice. He picked up Hank and placed him in one of the captain's chairs in the middle section of the taxi. He closed the door and drove as fast as he could to the hospital, which was only a few blocks away.

The driver stopped and ran inside the hospital and frantically called for help. Soon the paramedics removed Hank from the taxi and placed him on a stretcher. They rushed him inside and took him straight into surgery. The Iranian man looked in the backseat of his van and saw that blood was soaked into the seat. He looked down at his hands and saw blood on his fingers and under his fingernails. His clothes were also badly stained with blood. But he didn't care. His only concern was the wellbeing of the man in surgery.

The driver parked his taxi and went back inside to wait, wanting to make sure the guy he'd just rushed to the hospital would be okay.

"Excuse me, sir?" A lady at the front desk asked the Iranian man, "What is the name of the man you brought in?"

"I don't know," he replied in a thick Middle-Eastern accent. "He was unconscious when I found him."

The woman wrote down a few notes, and the Iranian taxi driver sat down in the waiting area. A few hours and two surgeries later, the doctor came out to let the taxi driver know that the man he had rescued would be okay. He also told him the man's name.

"His name's Hank, and I've seen his family in here before," the doctor explained. "They are new to this neighborhood, and he's the new foreman at the furniture factory up the street."

"Good," the taxi driver said in a tone of relief. It was almost as if he had been holding his breath for the past few hours. "I'm sure he has good insurance with a job like that. He will be okay."

"Actually, he's still in the probationary period and doesn't have insurance yet," the doctor said.

"If he doesn't have insurance, how is he going to pay?" the driver asked.

"We'll figure that out later. I'm sure his job is steady enough that he can make payments."

"You know, I'm sorry," the doctor continued. "I shouldn't

have told you any of that. I'm supposed to keep details like that confidential. Please don't let anyone know I said anything."

"Yes, sir," the taxi driver replied. "Did you let his family know?"

"Not yet. I'm going to track down their contact information in just a moment. I don't think they have a phone yet, but I'll send someone over to let them know."

"Let me go," the driver said. "I can pick them up and bring them here."

"Are you sure?" the doctor asked.

"Yes, absolutely."

The taxi driver got the address and left for Hank's house. *It's a good thing my taxi is a van*, he thought as he drove, *I don't know how big Hank's family is.* After finding Hank's home, he picked up Hank's wife and their three kids and drove them back to the hospital. After dropping them off at the hospital, he then drove to the bank, which was now open for the day.

The Iranian man had been working in the United States for several years, and he had saved up quite a bit of money. His goal was to move back to Iran and use the money to start a business. He withdrew $10,000 from his account and drove back to the hospital. He walked in and asked for the doctor.

"Here's $10,000," the taxi driver said. "This should pay for a lot of what you've done so far. If you need any more I will be back in a week to check on him. At that time, I can pay for what's left."

Somewhere around two thousand years ago, Jesus told a very similar story to that of the Middle-Eastern taxi driver. Here's a quick summary so you can see what I mean: One day, robbers attacked a man traveling between two cities and left him for dead at the side of the road. A priest and a Levite—two Jewish religious leaders—saw the bloodied man but refused to help him. Eventually, a Samaritan saw the man and saved his life. More than that, he generously covered all the man's expenses.

In order for us to understand this story and why Jesus told it, we need to consider its context.

One day, a lawyer stepped up to test Jesus, and asked: "Teacher, what must I do to inherit eternal life?" But instead of directly answering the question, Jesus asked him a question: "What does the Law say?"

The lawyer responded, " 'Love the Lord your God with all your heart and with all your soul and with all your strength and with all your mind'; and, 'Love your neighbor as yourself' " (Luke 10:27).

"That's right," Jesus responded. "Do this and you will live."

"But who is my neighbor?" the lawyer asked.

Jesus, in the brilliant way only He can, answered the man by telling him a story we know as the parable of the good Samaritan. The story is more than one of one man helping another in desperate need. It is a story full of nuance, and the hero of the story ends up being a perceived enemy of Israel. You see, the Jews of Jesus's time did not like the Samaritans but considered them traitors and half-breeds. The Samaritans' racial lineage wasn't pure, and they tried to worship God outside of Jerusalem. Yet a Samaritan, not a priest and not a Levite, was the hero of Jesus's story.

Biblical scholar Darrell Bock points out:

> Although the text gives us no reason [as to why the priest and Levite ignore the man] ... Jesus's point is, Simply be a neighbor. Do not rule out certain people as neighbors. And his parable makes the point emphatically by providing a model from a group the lawyer has probably excluded as possible neighbors. To love God means to show mercy to those in need. An authentic life is found in serving God and caring for others.... Neighbors are not determined by race, creed or gender; neighbors consist of anyone in need made in the image of God.[1]

In the last chapter, we discussed how the Greatest Commandment, which I nicknamed the Greatest Common Calling, is to love God with all we are. It's not a casual or half-hearted kind of love; it's an all-inclusive and completely absorbing pursuit of someone ultimate—God. I believe this love is the foundation for the Second Greatest Commandment—the Second Greatest Common Calling—which is our calling to love others as ourselves. In fact, I believe it is possible for us to love others as ourselves only if we first love God wholeheartedly.

Recently, I was reading the epistle to the Galatians when I noticed that the apostle Paul quoted the Second Greatest Common Calling when he wrote, "For the entire law is fulfilled in this one command: 'Love your neighbor as yourself.'" He then tells us that the only way we can do this is by walking in the Spirit: "Walk by the Spirit, and you will not gratify the desires of the flesh" (Galatians 5:16).But Paul doesn't stop there. He goes on to describe the difference between walking apart from the Spirit and walking in the Spirit, and then he concludes the section with a famous list: the fruit of the Spirit.

What is the first fruit listed? Do you remember? It is love. Clearly, Paul wants us to understand that the Spirit of God enables us to love others. The Second Greatest Common Calling—the call to love others—is possible only through the work of the Holy Spirit in our lives.

When I recognized the connection between love and the fruit of the Spirit, I decided to scan through 1 Corinthians 13, which is famously referred to as "the Love Chapter." Here is what Paul has to say about what real love looks like:

> Love is patient, love is kind. It does not envy, it does not boast, it is not proud. It does not dishonor others, it is not self-seeking, it is not easily angered, it keeps no record of wrongs. Love does not delight in evil but rejoices with the truth. It always protects, always trusts, always hopes, always perseveres. Love never fails. (vv. 4–8)

Yikes! Love is really hard, and I'm really bad at it. Sure, there are times when I'm patient and kind, but all the time? Yeah, right! Ask my wife. About the only aspects of love I've mastered so far are not boasting or being proud. Other than that, I'm sunk.

How are you doing with loving others? Are you ever rude to other people? Do you ever seek your own interests? Let's face it—loving others doesn't come naturally to us, yet it is our calling. That's why it's so important to realize that love is a fruit of the Spirit, which means God is the source of our ability to love others. In fact, have you ever noticed the connection between the fruit of the Spirit and 1 Corinthians 13? First, take a look at this list of the fruit of the Spirit from Galatians 5:22–23:

- Love
- Joy
- Peace
- Patience
- Kindness
- Goodness
- Faithfulness
- Gentleness
- Self-control

Now, let's take the fruit of the Spirit and place that list next to aspects of love as defined in 1 Corinthians 13:4–8. Here is what it looks like:

- The fruit of the Spirit is love: Love is patient.
- The fruit of the Spirit is joy: Love rejoices in the truth.
- The fruit of the Spirit is kindness: Love is kind; it doesn't boast.
- The fruit of the Spirit is peaceful: Love doesn't envy, isn't rude, isn't self-seeking.
- The fruit of the Spirit is gentle: Love isn't arrogant, love bears all things.
- The fruit of the Spirit is goodness: Love isn't arrogant.
- The fruit of the Spirit is self-control: Love isn't rude, isn't self-seeking.
- The fruit of the Spirit is faithfulness: Love bears all things, believes all things, hopes all things, endures all things, and never ends.

It's not an exact match, but these lists seem to go together, don't they? And this tells me that living in the love described in 1 Corinthians 13 is only possible through the work of the

Holy Spirit in our lives. In other words, the only way I can love God and love others is if the Holy Spirit does the work in and through me. And if that were to happen, it would change everything!

Can you imagine what our relationships would look like if we were able to avoid being rude, arrogant, envious, or boastful? Can you imagine what the world would be like if we Christians were consistently patient, kind, selfless, and hopeful? What do you think the church would look like if we truly loved one another the way the Bible describes?

I can tell you one thing, the church wouldn't be divided into a bunch of factions—it would be unified. In fact, I think this leads us to one of the common callings the Bible teaches: *We are called to unity.* Let's look at what this means.

A CALLING TO UNITY IN THE CHURCH

I can think of several historical speeches on the topic of unity, the most famous of which is probably Martin Luther King Jr.'s "I Have a Dream" speech. Yet none of the speeches I can think of comes close to comparing to one particular speech.

It was the beginning of one of the heaviest moments in human history. Night had fallen, yet it was darker than it appeared. On this particular evening, the darkness was sticky and thick—even suffocating. I can imagine that none of the normal sounds of night could be heard, that if you stepped outside any house, it would be eerily quiet.

In one particular house near a particular city park, a famous religious teacher was hanging out with his closest friends— well, *most* of his closest friends. One of the guys had already stepped out to take care of some mysterious business in town. Just a few minutes into dinner, the teacher had looked at him and told him to head out, which surprised everyone else. The guy's friends assumed that since he was in charge of the money, he must have been going to pick up more supplies for the party. One of the friends, however, had a different idea. He guessed that since it was Jesus who sent him out, he must be going to take care of some poor people they had noticed on the way in. Only Jesus knew the real reason Judas left, and He began to feel pressure as a result.

"Guys," Jesus said, "we don't have a lot of time left before I leave."

"That's okay," Peter chimed in, "we can leave too. Where are we going?"

"You can't go where I'm going, Peter. None of you can," Jesus explained.

"Ha-Ha! Right!" Peter said with a smirk. "Where would you possibly go that we can't go?"

Jesus didn't answer him but instead began to explain a bunch of stuff no one in the room could understand. It didn't make sense to them, but they all listened, asked questions, and then sat around feeling confused. I can picture Peter thinking of suggesting that Jesus go get some sleep for the night—He was obviously tired and not thinking clearly—but he didn't have a chance. After Jesus completed a long set of what the disciples saw as mumbo-jumbo, He began to pray.

The disciples were always amazed when Jesus prayed. He talked to God as if He was in the room with them—as if He was sitting at the table. Most of the time, they sat and listened quietly, and this situation was no different. As Jesus prayed, the disciples began to realize that He wasn't praying for just any-one—He was praying for *them* and for all people who would hear about Him as a result of the disciples work after He left them. It was a special moment, and the disciples felt as though they were a part of something much bigger than an evening dinner with Jesus.

> "Father, My dear Father, I'm not praying just for these guys in this room, although I do ask that You would set them apart and keep them safe. I'm praying for everyone else who will believe in Me because of the stories these guys will tell. You already know that their memories of our time together are going to be heard by millions of people over thousands of years and that many people will believe in Us as a result of them.
>
> And so, Daddy, I ask You to use these stories to make them one, as You and I are one. I want them to be uni-fied and bound together not only with each other but with Us, too. Father, don't just let them be unified in a shallow sense of the term—like those who are bound together over sports or political movements—but make them perfectly unified in love. Let them know how much I love them and how much You love them.
>
> May that love—the love We have for them—overflow into their love for one another. And may that love, the love You and I have for each other and for them, help them come together, put aside their own agendas and differ-ences, and be bound together through the Holy Spirit I'm sending them in just a few short weeks." (Paraphrase of John 17:20–26.)

Can you see why I believe Jesus's prayer that night is the greatest speech of all time on the subject of unity? I still can't come to grips with the idea that Jesus prayed for you and me— and for the millions of people who would live thousands of years later—to be unified. But Jesus knew we would struggle to be unified, so He prayed for us. It's the only time I can think of in which Jesus prayed for those—like you and me—who would hear the story later.

Obviously, unity is very important to God. Although the passage I paraphrased above doesn't read, "This is God's will for you ..." like many of the others we've discussed, Jesus's prayer makes it clear that we are called to live in unity with one another.

Other Scripture passages support this notion of the importance of unity. In Ephesians 4:1–6 we read:

> I urge you to live a life worthy of the calling you have received. Be completely humble and gentle; be patient, bearing with one another in love. Make every effort to keep the unity of the Spirit through the bond of peace. There is one body and one Spirit, just as you were called to one hope when you were called; one Lord, one faith, one baptism; one God and Father of all, who is over all and through all and in all.

The apostle Paul uses some very direct language in telling us that we are "called to one hope, one Lord, one faith, one baptism; one God and Father of all," and that calling is lived out through humility, gentleness, patience, bearing with one another in love (sounds a lot like the fruit of the Spirit and

1 Corinthians 13, doesn't it?), and pursuing "the unity of the Spirit through the bond of peace."

Let me ask you this: What do you think the "bond of peace" looks like in the body of Christ today? Furthermore, what can we do to pursue the unity of the body through the bond of peace?

For me, this means I need to begin moving past denominational boundaries, even if I stay connected to my chosen church—the Anglican Church. More than that, rather than arguing with my brothers and sisters in Christ over doctrinal differences, it means I'm going to refrain from saying negative things about denominations with whom I disagree. I know I will fail at this at times, but I have to make this my personal goal. Instead of arguing and criticizing, I'm going to choose to celebrate the beauty of each denomination. In fact, let me take a moment to describe some of the beauty I've personally witnessed in other denominations.

First, I grew up in a Southern Baptist church, where I learned many good lessons about God and His love for me. I first heard and responded to the gospel in a Southern Baptist church, so I can say that I'm a Christian today because of what God did through the SBC. And my Southern Baptist youth group sure made things fun! I learned that a passion for God isn't in contrast to enjoying life.

Second, I attended a multiracial church in college—and I think it may have been nondenominational. It sounds crazy now, but that church taught me that God and Jesus aren't white. My brain was aware of this, but this church helped me *understand* it. I also became best friends with a guy who wasn't white, and his passion for God changed, and continues to change, my perspective on important issues like race and what it means to grow up an ethnic minority.

After college, my wife and I attended a nondenominational hipster church that was also family friendly. Seriously, a church that is family friendly—one that lets kids stay in the service and doesn't look down on them (or us parents) when they make noise. Through this church, my wife and I learned that our faith journey was a *family* faith journey and not just an individual experience. Also, this church taught us that faith and art support each other and can work together.

My current church home is an Anglican congregation that emphasizes the importance of the family unit. In addition, this church has introduced me to the beauty and weight of historical liturgy and tradition. Through this church, I realized for the first time that the Christian faith isn't modern. Yes, it applies to our world today, but it is not a "new" faith. My brain knew Christianity was thousands of years old, but it never occurred to me that I could lean on church history and tradition as a way to further enrich my faith.

One final denominational experience: I also attended a nondenominational seminary, where I interacted with people from many different denominations and walks of life. This helped me to realize that I could disagree with people and yet still be friends with them. I often disagreed with people at school, but after getting to know them, I realized I needed to address disagreement in different ways. Instead of debating, we discussed deep issues with respect, love, and openness.

I know the word *openness* has a lot of baggage with it, but when I use that word, I'm not saying that I can be swayed from what I believe. Openness in this context means I respect people, especially people who see the world differently from the way I see it, enough to get to know them and realize they are smart and respectable and that their perspectives are worth being considered.

Over time, I've come to realize that appreciating the beauty of each denomination and having a healthy dose of openness to what smart and respectable friends believe leads to humility. And humility is a great equalizer, maybe the *greatest* equalizer. And here's something even better: It is also one of our primary common callings. Look at what Paul wrote on the subject of humility:

> So if there is any encouragement in Christ, any comfort from love, any participation in the Spirit, any affection and sympathy, complete my joy by being of the same mind, having the same love, being in full accord and of one mind. Do nothing from selfish ambition or conceit, but in humility count others more significant than yourselves. Let each of you look not only to his own interests, but also to the interests of others. Have this mind among yourselves, which is yours in Christ Jesus, who, though he was in the form of God, did not count equality with God a thing to be grasped, but emptied himself, by taking the form of a servant, being born in the likeness of men. And being found in human form, he humbled himself by becoming obedient to the point of death, even death on a cross. (PHILIPPIANS 2:1–8 ESV)

The call to humility in this passage is a call to be like Christ, who defined humility through His obedience to the Father and

His sacrifice for us. Notice that it contains some of the themes we've already discussed in this chapter:

- First, there are the references to *love* and *joy* in this passage.
- Second, notice the emphasis on unity, which Paul defines as having the same mind, same love, and being in one accord with one another.
- Third, this passage also defines an important aspect of humility: obedience to God the Father by desiring what's in the best interests of others and then doing it.

This brings us to where we will pick up in the next chapter: What does it look like to answer God's common calling to put aside our own desires and do what's in the best interests of others.

A Common Calling to Live Intentionally

All Thoughts, all Passions, all Delights,
Whatever stirs this mortal Frame,
All are but Ministers of Love,
And feed his sacred flame.
—WILLIAM WORDSWORTH, "Love"

His name was James, but his mom called him "Beans."

He had long brown hair, sported hippy-style glasses, and wore a tie-dye peace shirt. I met him on top of a mountain— well, almost at the top. I had parked at a scenic pull-off on the Blue Ridge Parkway in North Carolina, and I was alternating between looking at the view and reading my Bible. It had been a really long week at work, and I needed some time to breathe before jumping back into the marathon of personnel problems I had been dealing with.

The view was working.

The weight of issues slowly faded, and the fresh mountain air soothed me. That was going on in my body and soul when a man walked up to my truck.

"Is the visitor center close to here?" he asked.

"Sure is. Only two more miles and you're there," I responded.

"Thank you so much," he replied.

"You're welcome," I answered.

I finished reading and started up my red Chevy truck to head to work. The man had made it just 100 yards or so in his walk toward the center, and he seemed to be walking slowly on purpose. He struck me as the kind of guy who liked to take his time and enjoy every moment of every day.

I felt like I should offer him a ride.

At first, I came up with four or five legitimate reasons why I shouldn't help. I didn't want to be late to work. I didn't want to take the chance he'd kill me and steal my truck. You know, things worth thinking about. None of my excuses stuck, however, especially when I thought about how ironic it would be to be robbed and murdered by a guy in a tie-dye peace shirt.

The road was pretty empty, so I pulled up next to him and rolled down the window.

"You want a ride down the mountain?" I asked.

"That would be great!" he answered.

He opened the door and climbed into the passenger seat. I don't know if I should admit it, but he smelled bad, so I rolled down the windows. "Don't worry," I lied, and said it was because I enjoyed the cool mountain air.

"Were you reading your Bible?" the man asked me.

"Sure was," I said. "By the way, I'm Daniel."

"I'm Beans, and it's nice to meet you."

"Beans?" I asked. "Is that a nickname or your real name?"

"It's a nickname. My dad named me James, but my mom doesn't like that name so she called me 'Beans.' I don't really like James either, so I just tell people my name's Beans."

"That's kind of funny."

"It sure is."

"Where are you from?"

"Alabama, originally. That's where I grew up. I'm not homeless, you know. I'm home-free!" he said with a smile.

"What's the difference?"

"Homeless people are those who struggle to find work or have problems that keep them from getting their feet under them." Beans explained. "I'm home-free because I don't want to be tied down. I've actually worked a lot, but I don't want to be bound to a mortgage or anything like that."

I don't want to be bound to a mortgage either, I thought, *but I'd rather have a mortgage than be home-free.*

"I like the Bible," Beans said, bringing the conversation back to where it started. "What were you reading?"

"I was reading about creation and how God built enough evidence of His existence into the world that mankind doesn't have any excuse not to believe in Him."

"I don't understand how anyone can say there isn't a God," Beans offered. "There's no way you can look at this world and suggest anything other than that someone with a powerful imagination could come up with this place. That's one of the two things that bugs me the most!"

"What's the other thing?" I asked.

"When people try to tell me their religion's the only one. Who are they to say they have it all figured out?"

Normally, when I hear someone say something like that, I search for a way to challenge it. But that didn't feel right in this situation. Something in my spirit—I think it was the Holy Spirit—kept me from stirring up a debate.

"Would you mind taking me to Ingles?" Beans asked regarding a supermarket in town. "I heard they have great dumpsters. Being home-free is great in regard to bills, but when you travel to a new city—like I am today—and haven't had a chance to work, it can leave you pretty hungry. But you wouldn't believe all the stuff they throw away. One of the guys I know from around here said the Ingles on Tunnel Road is the best one for finding quality food in the dumpsters. So that's where I'm headed. Even if you can't get me the whole way, I'd be thankful for as close as you can get me."

"It's not that far," I replied. "I can take you the whole way."

I gave him a ride to Ingles Market, which was only a few miles past the visitor center. We talked about creation, God, and the Bible for nearly the entire ten-minute drive. Bean's obvious amazement at God encouraged me, and I think I was able to encourage him a little bit too. We got to Ingles, and I felt the Lord prompt me to give him some cash so he could buy some food. I don't usually give homeless—I'm sorry, *home-free*—people money, but I trusted him to use the cash for exactly what he said he would—fried chicken.

"Thank you for the ride!" Beans said as he got out of the truck. "It was really nice to talk to you."

"You're welcome," I responded.

As Beans closed the door, the Lord prompted me to give him the Bible we had been talking about for the past few minutes. "Do you have a Bible?" I asked.

"I don't."

I handed him my Bible.

"I can't take that!" he said. "You obviously like that book because you've been talking about it a lot."

"You sure can take it," I responded. "I've got Bibles, and this one is particularly well put together. I think you'll like it. What I like about this one is that it's written in a more modern language, which makes it easier to read."

"Oh man! That sounds great. Sometimes the Bible is too complicated with the old language and stuff. This means so much to me; I will be sure to read it." Beans thanked me again and walked away. I believed him. I think he really did read that Bible.

I'm not sure who was more encouraged from our discussion, but I know that God had set up the entire thing.

MOVING BEYOND GOOD INTENTIONS

We ended the last chapter with a question: What does it look like to put aside our own desires and to practice the type of humility that puts others' interests above our own?

In my situation with Beans, it meant putting aside both my fear of being robbed and the inconvenience of being a few minutes late to work and giving him a ride to the grocery store. It wasn't natural for me to do this, and I had a list of excuses. But God the Holy Spirit pushed me past my excuses to obedience. It also took intentionality on my part, which in this instance meant I had to *force* myself to stop and offer a ride. I could have done what I do most of the time and convinced myself not to help. I could have stopped at the good idea to help, even the *desire* to serve, and driven away without assisting Beans. It took an intentional act of obedience, something I think the Holy Spirit helps us with, to move past good intentions and actually help the home-free hippy from Alabama.

I've learned that intentionality is vital to putting most of God's common callings into practice. In my last book, *Ten Days Without*, I wrote a lot about the difference between people who make a difference in the world and those who don't. The difference-makers, I've learned, live lives of obedience to God and follow through on their good intentions. It's easy for us to *want* to help someone, but following through and actually helping someone . . . now that's hard!

If we're going to do this—if we are going to live out our faith through obedience to the common callings of God—it's going to take intentionality.

Let's look at a few more common callings to see why that is true.

CALLED TO MAKE DISCIPLES

The most famous passage I can think of regarding the call to make disciples is found in the gospel of Matthew:

> Therefore go and make disciples of all nations, baptizing them in the name of the Father and of the Son and of the Holy Spirit, and teaching them to obey everything I have commanded you. And surely I am with you always, to the very end of the age. (28:19–20)

Nearly all Christians agree that God wants us to share the gospel and make disciples, but there is much discussion on how this should be done. Should we preach on the street? Should we come up with catchy ways to debate people into the kingdom? Should we design and write clever tracts? Should we simply live out our Christian life in front of people so they see our faith and ask us about it? Should we glue Bibles to our fore-heads and plaster fish stickers on the back of our pants? Okay, maybe not the last one, but some of the others are considered legitimate tools for sharing the gospel.

Most of my family, and most of my wife's family for that matter, are evangelists in the "go find a stranger and share the gospel" kind of way. They believe that this answers the call found in Matthew 28 and is the first step in making disciples. That's not how I am, however. I feel really uncomfortable with the idea of walking up to a stranger in the street and asking him if he is going to heaven when he dies.

My conviction is that God has surrounded me with rela-tionships, and it's within the context of those relationships that I should share the gospel. I see the Great Commission, as the passage in Matthew 28 is often titled, as relational, meaning I believe that moving past sharing the gospel to actually making full-blown disciples starts with building interpersonal relation-ships with other people. I believe this so deeply that I moved my family back to Asheville to try and intentionally live out God's Great Commission.

A few years ago, I realized something. Each week, I spent more time with my coworkers than with anyone else. Once I factored in sleep, I realized that I spent nearly as much time with people at work as I did with my wife and kids (not nec-essarily a good thing). More than that, I realized that most of the opportunities I had to influence others came in work set-tings—at lunch, getting coffee, or waiting for an event to start.

A few months after this realization hit me, I happened to be looking for a new job. I was being considered for a pastoral position at a church. It looked like I was going to get it, and my wife and I planned to accept the job. But as I prayed about it, thought about it, and sought wise counsel about it, I became more and more uncomfortable with the idea of accepting the job. I was convicted that my becoming a pastor would separate me from the people with whom I needed to spend time. I wanted to influence people for Christ, and I wanted to work in a job where I could spend time with people who didn't go to church.

So I moved—I mean *we* moved. My wife and I moved back to North Carolina so I could spend my time with people who weren't in church. Now, I didn't feel "called" to work in the business world, and I didn't return to North Carolina because I thought I had found my "dream job." I came back to try to make disciples—to share the gospel and to help people see that it affects every area of their lives. I didn't want to become a pastor who tells the people in his congregation they can be in a secular job and still do ministry. I wanted to be a guy in a secular job who daily tries to figure out how Christianity meshes with the real world.

So I'm doing it. Right now, it still feels like an experiment, and I'm not very good at it. But I'm trying. My prayer every morning is for God to give me the eyes to see and the ears to hear what He would have me do within the context in which He has placed me. So far, that's the best I can come up with as to what it means to live missionally and make disciples.

Please don't read this story as a critique of pastoral ministry. God knows I'm not suggesting that my way is the best way or the only way. I just want my story to encourage those who don't feel called to pastoral ministry or the mission field. Fulltime pastoral ministry is vitally important; it's just not for me at this point in my life (only God knows if that may be in my future).

My point is that I think we can disagree on the mode of "making disciples" while agreeing that we are called to do it. For me, this means working at a family entertainment center and hotel for now. For you ... well, I don't know how God wants you to make disciples. I just know He wants you do so, and that it is going to take some intentionality on your part to make it happen.

CALLED TO LOOK AFTER THOSE IN NEED

I don't know if you've noticed, but God seems to care a lot about vulnerable people. The Bible contains many examples of both providing for the defenseless and of God calling His people to care for them. Although we are going to look at three specific needy groups God often mentions in Scripture, I think it's important to note that these are not the only vulnerable people in the world. I think we are called to help *all* the groups, even though God mentions just a few specifically.

Consider the following verses:

Defend the weak and the fatherless;
     uphold the cause of the poor and the oppressed.
Rescue the weak and the needy;
     deliver them from the hand of the wicked.
     (Psalm 82:3–4)

Although this passage specifically mentions orphans—whom we are going to talk about specifically in just a moment—it also mentions other groups of vulnerable people. This means

God calls us to look after the weak, the poor, the oppressed, and the needy.

In our culture and world today, who are the weak? Who are the oppressed? Who are the needy? And how can we help those people? How can we "defend," "uphold the cause of," "rescue," and "deliver" them? Maybe it would be helpful to make a list of vulnerable people—people you might be able to help.

I'm going to stop here for a moment and preach to myself. I'm going to get back to groups of vulnerable people in a moment, but first I'd like to share my personal confession:

I have spent hours trying to figure out what I'm supposed to do with my life. I've spent hours researching majors and colleges, reading books, listening to podcasts about discovering a dream job and finding God's calling. Yet I've spent very little time intentionally thinking about how I can follow God's call to defend, uphold, rescue, and deliver those who are vulnerable. It's time my priorities shifted from myself, time that I take on the spirit of humility Christ wore when He obeyed God and died for you and me, and time that I begin prioritizing the calling God has placed on my life—the same call He's placed on all believers to love our vulnerable neighbors and consider their needs before our own.

Please excuse me for that, but writing this chapter has been very convicting to me. Protecting those who need protecting and providing for those who need help seems like such a simple calling from God, yet I've never thought much about the weak and the needy. So there's my confession.

Not only have I neglected the poor, oppressed, and weak but I've also spent very little time caring for the groups of people God talks about the most in Scripture. If you do a quick search for verses about "orphans" or "the fatherless," "widows," and "foreigners," you will find a long list of references, many of which mention all three groups together.

God cares deeply and specifically about those who are most vulnerable. To see just how deeply He cares, take a look at the following verses:

- "He defends the cause of the fatherless and the widow, and loves the foreigner residing among you, giving them food and clothing" (DEUTERONOMY 10:18)
- "The LORD protects the strangers; He supports the fatherless and the widow, but He thwarts the way of the wicked" (PSALM 146:9 NASB).

There are many more passages showing us how much God cares about the most vulnerable, but these two give us a feel for God's love and compassion for them. What's more, if you search for these groups in the Bible, you will also find several references calling us to join God in His work of defending the defenseless:

- "Learn to do good; seek justice, reprove the ruthless, defend the orphan, plead for the widow" (ISAIAH 1:17 NASB).
- "Religion that God our Father accepts as pure and fault-less is this: to look after orphans and widows in their distress and to keep oneself from being polluted by the world" (JAMES 1:27)

God cares about the vulnerable, and He wants us to care about them too. But it's not always easy to do so, especially today, when we live in a political climate that is so divided over issues of foreigners and strangers, in other words, immigrants. Yet in Deuteronomy 10:18, God tells His people that He loves the foreigners living among them, and by extension He wants us to love them too.

I believe this call to love the foreigners among us includes two groups that have been prominent in the news over the past several years: immigrants from the south and immigrants from the Middle East. Don't you believe the passages informing us of God's compassion for the stranger and foreigner should inform the way we Christians approach the issue of immigration? Shouldn't it impact our perspective on Muslims, Mexicans, and other immigrants living in our country?

God's Word is very clear that we are to help the strangers living among us, even if they are from the Middle East. Part of me wishes we could pick and choose who God cares about, but we asked Him for His calling and His will for our lives, and He seems to be pretty clear on this point: "Do not mistreat them … love [the foreigner who resides among you in your land]" (Leviticus 19:33–34); provide food for them (Leviticus 19:9–10); do not oppress them (Exodus 23:9); do not deprive them of justice (Malachi 3:5); and invite them [the stranger] in (Matthew 25:25–36).

If you and I take to heart what God says about caring for the most vulnerable among us, if we attempt to intentionally live out what God is calling us to do, then we may likely be unpopular with some people in our families. Some of our friends may not agree with us, and they may stop being our friends because of it.

I don't want to get into an argument about open borders

versus closed borders or about the proper vetting of immigrants—that's not what this is about. But I think we can all agree, regardless of what side we're on, that the above verses should inform our approach to those who are now here with us.

Please do not take this as my support for the positions of any particular political party. Although in the past I was tied to a party, I'm not anymore. I don't think a biblical perspective on issues like immigration lends itself to only aligning ourselves with any one group of people. Although we can avoid political arguments on these issues, we can't avoid a very clear common calling to take care of the vulnerable—especially foreigners.

At the same time, however, we shouldn't focus so much on foreigners and immigrants that we forget to also care for other vulnerable groups of people mentioned in the Bible, specifically orphans and widows.

In our churches and in our communities are many women and men who have lost spouses and many children who have been left fatherless. The question for all of us is this: what can we do to serve and support these vulnerable people? What can we do to look after them? What intentional steps can we take to meet their needs?

From an individual perspective, there are many ways to look after orphans and at-risk children. At one point in my life, this meant living in Romania for three months and ministering to kids who lived in orphanages. For a friend of mine, caring for orphans meant adopting a baby girl from China. My sister became a social worker so she could pursue her passion of helping defenseless kids living in terrible situations. And one of my seminary professors spent much of his career developing support materials and a list of practices his students can use to care for at-risk children as they begin their churches and ministries.

From a church perspective, there are many ways for congregations to care for orphans and children at risk. I've heard of congregations challenging the church to adopt kids out of the foster care system. For example, one congregation in Alabama made quite an impact on the system and saw many kids adopted and cared for. When I lived in Colorado Springs, my small group connected with an organization that provides licensed childcare for foster parents so they can get away for a date night. I've also heard of congregations collecting school supplies or feeding homeless children in their communities.

Regarding widows and widowers, there are many ways to help. Childcare and mentoring can be especially helpful to single parents. Also, think about how important companionship is for those who lose a spouse. Widows and widowers alike need friends to be available to support them emotionally, financially, and spiritually.

The truth is, all of us are surrounded by opportunities to support orphans and widows. We simply need to intentionally shape our lives and our thinking and look around and ask God specifically what He would have us do.

A CALL TO SEEK JUSTICE

In the Old Testament book of Micah, we find another well-known passage that outlines another common calling, that of seeking justice for the vulnerable among us: "What does the

LORD require of you? To act justly and to love mercy and to walk humbly with your God" (Micah 6:8).

In the last section, we touched on the issue of justice when we discussed our treatment of foreigners, widows, and orphans. But Micah tells God's people that they are called to the cause of justice for other groups as well. Evidently, God's people during Micah's time had neglected some of those groups or had gone the extra step in the wrong direction by treating them unfairly.

I sometimes like to read a particular verse or passage in several different translations so I can get the feel for the scope of how a passage has been translated over the years. If you look up Micah 6:8 in different translations, you will find some variation in the New International Version phrase "to act justly." Here are two examples: "to do justly" (KJV) and "to promote justice" (NET).

Although these translations are similar, they each bring a slightly different angle to the cause of justice. Yet even within the varying scope of this common calling, all the translations make one thing clear: the call to justice is active, not passive. Regardless of which Bible translation you pick up, you can see that we are called to "act," "do," or "promote"—meaning we are called to action. In other words, if we are going to live out this common calling, we will need to be intentional about it. We will have to move past the *desire* to make a difference in issues of injustice and actively participate in *promoting* justice.

So what would promoting justice and acting justly look like today? How does this common call transform the way you and I live as we seek to do God's will? I'm by no means an expert on issues of justice, but I will share a few things I think we can agree on.

First, justice is colorblind, meaning that this common call includes justice for all races, nations, and people groups. Whether it's genocide in Rwanda, refugees in the Middle East, or men and women of color in the inner city, God wants us to seek justice for all of them. This colorblind justice includes an ability to see past our own skin color as well. In other words, we can't side with a particular people group or take a stance on a particular story on the news just because we have the same color skin they do. Seeking justice means seeking the truth for everyone involved.

In the last chapter, I wrote about my experience attending a multiracial church when I was in college. The best thing to come out of attending that church was my relationship with a black man named Ben, who became one of my best friends.

Ben and I met often at Chick-fil-A to spend time together and discuss life issues. After several months of hanging out with Ben, I finally came to the place where I felt comfortable asking him a question that had been on my mind for many years.

"Ben," I asked, "does racism still exist? I'm asking you because where I come from, I don't see it. Then again, I'm a white guy from a mostly white high school and a mostly white church. I see stories on the news that racism is still around, but I've not experienced it, nor have I known friends—many of whom are also men and women of color—who have experienced it. So I want to know, is the news making this stuff up to get us to watch TV? Or does racism still exist?"

Ben thought a moment before answering. One of the things I like about Ben is that he's different from me in that he doesn't cast a gut response on people. He's calculated, and he thinks before he speaks. I could tell he had a lot to say, but I knew he also wanted to be careful.

"A few years ago, someone came to our house, stole a bunch of stuff off our porch, and spray-painted racial slurs on our house," Ben told me. "My mom and dad have been treated rudely many times in various retail stores. And every once in a while, people make jokes about slavery just loud enough for us to overhear them. Does that mean racism is still as evident and pervasive as it was a few decades ago? Of course not. But does racism still exist? Unfortunately, I think it does because my family has experienced it."

That day, my perspective shifted because I trust Ben. To me, he wasn't a random guy being interviewed on the news. He was my best friend, and he had experiences I couldn't ignore.

Recently, the United States of America has been embroiled in several racial controversies. If you take the news for face value (which is almost never a good idea, by the way), it might appear that a large number of white cops are out shooting black men and that a large number of black men are out ambushing and killing white cops. You'd think we were back to the days of Martin Luther King Jr. and the KKK. Although we have only information that has been reported to us—information that is often wrong and inaccurate—the fact that these incidents are taking place at all shows that an inherent level of injustice still exists in our culture. It shows that all is not right.

Justice is colorblind, and God is calling you and me to act justly every day. Those of us in the US have opportunities right in front of us to act justly. So how will we respond?

Maybe a first step for you could be to take the time to talk with your friends who are from different racial backgrounds.

I'm not talking about just white and black but also friends who are Hispanic, Native American, Chinese, or Indian, and ask them about their experiences. Ask them how you can promote justice for them.

A few other ways to live out the call of justice, and this is on more of a global level, include connecting with organizations like International Justice Mission or other nonprofits that focus on discovering and eradicating injustice in the world.

Here are just a few other forms of injustice that are taking place right now as you read this book. (Don't believe me? Check the sources in the back of the book.)

1. There are more slaves in the world right now than during the transatlantic slave trade.[2]

2. Millions of children are trapped in the commercial sex trade.[3]

3. In many African countries, orphans and widows are having houses, land, and personal property stolen from them; and the governments of those countries are refusing to get it back for them. (This is called "land-grabbing.")[4]

4. There are places in the world where police officers grab random people and beat them up until they admit to a crime they didn't commit. The police have pressure on them to solve cases and are regularly "solving" these cases by arresting people who aren't guilty.[5]

There is so much injustice in the world, and you and I have many opportunities to get involved. I don't know which of these examples connects with you, but I would encourage you to think about what you can do to fight the injustices you see in the world around you.

A CALL TO CARE FOR OUR BROTHERS AND SISTERS

We have already covered several common callings in this chapter, so I will not go into as much detail on the next few. But if we're serious about discovering God's call for our lives, we will need to consider the following callings as well:

Called to Deal with Our Own Sin First

God calls us Christians to deal first with our own sin before we try to help others move past the blind spots in their lives. In Matthew 7, Jesus says, "first take the plank out of your own eye, and then you will see clearly to remove the speck from your brother's eye" (v. 5). In other words, don't judge your brother or sister with an attitude that you're squeaky clean and haven't sinned. Instead, take on the spirit of humility we talked about in the last chapter, deal with the sin in your life, and then help your brothers or sisters deal with their blind spots.

Here are a few questions to ask yourself as you try to live out this important principle:

1. What is my relationship with this person? Does our relationship have the capacity to deal with this issue?

2. If I'm going to confront sin in my brother or sister's life, am I ready to deal with and respond to the criticism this situation will bring on me?

3. Why do I feel I need to confront this issue? Is it a

genuine problem of morality? Or am I being picky in my preferences?

Called to Help Meet Needs in the Church

The apostle James tells us that we are called to meet the physical needs of our brothers and sisters in Christ: "Suppose a brother or a sister is without clothes and daily food. If one of you says to them, 'Go in peace; keep warm and well fed,' but does nothing about their physical needs, what good is it?" (James 2:15–16).

Think about it this way: What if you found out my sister hadn't eaten in three days, and she had come to me for help. You discover that instead of giving her food, I told her I loved her and hoped she would be okay. What would you think of me? That's the kind of situation James is describing.

The apostle John echoed this point when he wrote, "If anyone has material possessions and sees a brother or sister in need but has no pity on them, how can the love of God be in that person?" (1 John 3:17).

In the kingdom of God that Jesus proclaimed and represented here on earth, we are no longer only defined by our bloodline. Instead, believers are now a part of a larger family, the universal family of God. As a result, we now have a bunch of new relatives who are not connected to us through a bloodline, but instead through a shared faith in Jesus.

James and John are both making the point that we need to treat our spiritual family in the same way we treat our family bloodline. You and I wouldn't think of not providing for our siblings if they were in need. I have three younger sisters, and if they were without clothes or food I would do whatever I had to do to take care of them.

James and John are challenging those of us in the family of God to provide for one another's physical needs with the same fervency. For example, if we find out a family in our local church doesn't have enough money for school supplies, we should go buy them. If we know of a single mom who is struggling to put food on the table, we should buy groceries for her. And if we find out that a family is without the clothes they need, whether it's a uniform for school or the right clothes for PE, we should do our part and buy them clothes.

What opportunities to provide for people in your church are you aware of? In what ways could you provide for your spiritual brothers or sisters today?

Called to Treat All People Equally

You and I are called to treat everybody the same. My dad used to tell his employees, "We all put our pants on the same way." In business, people often get stuck on their job title. They think that achieving a certain level of authority or responsibility means they no longer have to clean bathrooms or pick up trash. So my dad likes to remind his leaders that no job or task is too small for them—after all, the executives and the support staff all get dressed the same way.

Speaking through the apostle James, God calls us to treat people with the same attitude with which my dad treats his employees—that no one is more important than anyone else:

My brothers and sisters, believers in our glorious Lord Jesus Christ must not show favoritism. Suppose a man comes into your meeting wearing a gold ring and fine clothes, and a poor man in filthy old clothes also comes in. If you show special attention to the man wearing fine clothes and say, "Here's a good seat for you," but say to the poor man, "You stand there" or "Sit on the floor by my feet," have you not discriminated among yourselves and become judges with evil thoughts?

Listen, my dear brothers and sisters: Has not God chosen those who are poor in the eyes of the world to be rich in faith and to inherit the kingdom he promised those who love him? But you have dishonored the poor. Is it not the rich who are exploiting you? Are they not the ones who are dragging you into court? Are they not the ones who are blaspheming the noble name of him to whom you belong? If you really keep the royal law found in Scripture, "Love your neighbor as yourself," you are doing right. (JAMES 2:1–8)

Not only does this calling apply to a business setting but it also applies to how we treat celebrities or other famous people. Recently, a few of our team members—a group of eighteen-year-old guys working go-carts—discovered that a certain famous actor and comedian was in line at the indoor go-cart track. It was almost funny to watch the way they fawned over this guy and tried to make his experience seamless and perfect. Unfortunately, these guys do not put the same amount of effort into making all other guests feel the same way. But what if they did? What if they treated every guest as if he or she were a celebrity?

I think what James is driving at is this: It's not wrong to treat the wealthy man with respect and kindness, but we also need to treat everyone else in the same manner.

—◇—

As you can see, the Bible has a lot to say about the subject of God's calling for your life. We've barely scratched the surface of all the common callings found in Scripture. Perhaps this discussion of them will drive you to the Bible to find other things God calls each of us to do. The key is never to forget this: we live by God's grace and we serve out of our love for Him, not by a checklist of dos and don'ts.

But before we end our discussion on God's will, I want to consider two other common callings that have completely changed my perspective on God's will for my life. I think they may help you too.

CHAPTER NINE

A Common Calling to Overcome Fear and Love Our Enemies

Turning and turning in the widening gyre
The falcon cannot hear the falconer;
Things fall apart; the centre cannot hold;
Mere anarchy is loosed upon the world,
The blood-dimmed tide is loosed, and everywhere
The ceremony of innocence is drowned;
The best lack all conviction, while the worst
Are full of passionate intensity.
—WILLIAM BUTLER YEATS, "The Second Coming"

I imagine it was like any normal day, because that's usually how people seem to describe the moments before "things fall apart" and "mere anarchy is loosed upon the world," to quote Yeats. It was the beginning of fall in Pennsylvania, and most of the leaves were still green. The nighttime temperatures hinted that the seasons were changing, and I'm sure the anticipation of autumn beauty was building in many residents of Lancaster County.

In a single-room schoolhouse—a quaint white building with a bell on top—a group of schoolchildren had gathered for another day of class. The teacher, along with a few adult helpers, was already well into the rhythm of another school day when a man—a familiar man, the local milkman—walked into the school.

But he was not carrying milk bottles. He was carrying guns.

The man asked the adults and the boys to leave the room, and then he commanded ten girls to lie down on the floor in front of the chalkboard, which was likely already filled with the day's lessons. A few minutes later, gunshots could be heard from outside the schoolhouse. The police rushed in to find the girls injured, many of them mortally, and the man dead. By the end of the day, five young girls died from gunshot wounds. It was an act of evil in the most unlikely of places—an Amish farm community. Yeats's words are so appropriate here: "The ceremony of innocence is drowned."

Many years after the school shooting in Pennsylvania, during an evening prayer service at Emanuel African Methodist Episcopal Church in downtown Charleston, South Carolina, a young man walked in and shot ten people, killing nine of them, including the senior pastor. The man—a racist—was later charged with hate crimes, convicted, and sentenced to be executed.

There's something these two stories have in common, and it's more than the obvious connections of guns, violence, and evil. Yes, both of these events are marked with infamy. Yes, both stories include unspeakable evil and horror. But both groups of people—the Amish in Pennsylvania and the AME congregation in Charleston—transformed the story lines from unspeakable evil to unimaginable forgiveness.

According to Lancaster, Pennsylvania's tourism blog, just hours (not weeks, or even days) after the attack, the Amish began proclaiming unconditional grace and forgiveness to the shooter's family.[1] Here's the timeline of that day from the site:

> In the midst of their grief over this shocking loss, the people of the Amish community didn't cast blame, they didn't point fingers, they didn't hold a press conference with attorneys at their sides. Instead, they reached out with grace and compassion toward the killer's family.
>
> The afternoon of the shooting an Amish grandfather of one of the girls who was killed expressed forgiveness toward the killer, Charles Roberts. That same day Amish neighbors visited the Roberts' family to comfort them in their sorrow and pain.
>
> Later that week the Roberts' family was invited to the funeral of one of the Amish girls who had been killed. And Amish mourners outnumbered the non-Amish at Charles Roberts' [the shooter's] funeral.[2]

In Charleston, a similar storyline emerged as many of the families and relatives of those who had died offered forgiveness to the attacker. A year later, when they were offered the opportunity to confront the man responsible for the deaths of their family members, people like Nadine Collier proclaimed forgiveness and mercy.[3] She was the daughter of Ethel Lance, who was murdered by the racist, yet she forgave her mother's killer.

There are many other stories in which forgiveness is offered to someone who doesn't deserve it, but these two stand out. Both stories stand in stark contrast to many other stories of hate crimes and evil we've witnessed over the past few years. The story line of these two incidents changed. The news reports were no longer focused exclusively on the evil that had transpired; instead, reporters began covering remarkable stories of compassion and forgiveness.

We live in a culture of fear, don't we? Think about how many shootings, how many horrifying acts of evil, we've been exposed to in news reports just in the past few years.

Aside from fears of physical harm—like shootings, terrorism, and other forms of violence—our culture often focuses on many other fears as well. Both liberals and conservatives fill blogs, radio shows, and cable news programs with fearful predictions of what will happen to the country if the wrong leaders are put in charge. Religious leaders fill the airwaves with dismay and hopelessness as they discuss what they consider the slippage of morality and ethics in our culture. And finally, nearly everyone I know has expressed fear over the economy or how they will make a living. Whether they are physical, political, cultural, or economic, our world today offers much that can lead to paralyzing fear.

But Christians are not called to live in fear but are actually called to the opposite: "So do not fear, for I am with you; do not be dismayed, for I am your God. I will strengthen you and help you; I will uphold you with my righteous right hand" (Isaiah 41:10).

Our calling to live our lives free of the crippling effects of fear doesn't mean we won't sometimes struggle with fear and a lack of hope. Even David—a king nicknamed "the man after God's own heart"—struggled with fear and dismay in the midst of troubling circumstances. "Why, my soul, are you downcast?" he wrote. "Why so disturbed within me? Put your hope in God, for I will yet praise him, my Savior and my God" (Psalm 42:11).

What David seems to be alluding to in this verse, and what we must recognize, is that when fear is more prominent in our lives than hope, then something is wrong. Our faith is not intrinsically fearful; it is foundationally hopeful. If we allow ourselves to live in fear over where our culture is headed or if we promote fear in regard to political candidates, the economy, or threats of terrorism, then we are caught up in a perspective outside of what God offers us in Isaiah 41 and Psalm 42. When that happens, we will not be filled with the hope that comes from trusting in God, but our souls will be downcast, fearful, and dismayed.

So since being downcast and fearful is outside of who God has called us to be, how are we as Christians called to respond to political uncertainty, cultural decline, economic upheaval, and physical violence? I believe the answer to that question can be found in the common callings you'll see as you read the remainder of this chapter.

CALLED TO RESPECT ALL
POLITICAL AUTHORITY

The year I turned sixteen was also an election year—a very important election year. The two presidential candidates seemed to represent more than just their political parties. There was a strong religious overtone to the election, and a powerful group of evangelical Christian leaders banded together through radio shows, newsletters, and sermons to promote one candidate from one party.

I remember hearing, and buying into, how important this particular election was in regard to religious freedom and preserving our nation's Christian values. I may have only been a naïve sixteen-year-old, but I was convinced that the outcome of this election would somehow directly impact the outcome of Christianity. I started believing it was up to me—and a particular political party—to defend the faith. In my mind, if this party lost, then God had lost.

So I did what I could do to help. Because I was only sixteen, I couldn't vote. But there was something else I could do. I had a green Jeep Cherokee Sport I could drive off-road, so I started swerving off the road to drive over political signs that supported the other party. If I couldn't get to a sign with my Jeep, I would stop and steal the signs from the side of the road and throw them in the back of my vehicle. As the election drew closer, I had compiled a large enough stack of signs to invite my friends over for a bonfire. Not only had I been effective in either removing or driving over political signs, but also my actions had inspired others, and they too brought signs they had collected to the bonfire. We were all so proud of ourselves, especially after the candidate we supported—the man we believed would be solely responsible for protecting and defending Christianity—won the election. To us, it seemed like God had won.

Interestingly enough, the outcome of this election would later be labeled the peak of power for the religious right. But many of us—myself included—later became discouraged and frustrated as we watched this president over the following eight years. It was not because he was a bad guy, but because there was no way he could live up to our foolish expectations. At the time, we didn't realize that the President of the United States is not the defender of Christianity and God. God can take care of himself.

Eight years later, the party that had been in power—the party I thought would save the world—lost, and a new president was sworn in. Many of the same Christian leaders who had supported the previous president spoke out against this man, but he won anyway. My political framework began to crack. My hope in politics began to fade.

I was left with questions I hadn't yet considered. What happens when "our" candidate loses? Does God lose? Of course not! In fact, I think the Bible suggests that God is just as active in a result that doesn't go our way as He is when the person we want is elected. Paul wrote, "Let everyone be subject to the governing authorities, for there is no authority except that which God has established. The authorities that exist have been established by God" (Romans 13:1).

As much as we may not want to admit it, there's no differentiation in Romans 13 about who gets elected or which party affiliation they hold. It doesn't say God establishes good

WHAT TO DO WHEN YOU DON'T KNOW WHAT TO DO

leaders and Satan establishes everyone else. It says God puts authority in power, and it tells us that it is His will that we respect and be subject to whoever that person is.

But what does respecting authority look like? What does it mean to be subject to a president or party we don't agree with? I'm not 100 percent sure, but I do know this: I've said a few things that would fall outside the definition of "respect" for the authority God has established. In fact, I've said a few things that were *very* disrespectful. And here's the crazy thing: When I've disrespected the person in authority, I've disrespected God's choice. Ouch!

I'm not saying we shouldn't get involved in politics or that we should abstain from voting. I don't think it's wrong to criticize the decisions of someone who seems to make the wrong decisions. I think God has given us an opportunity to be involved in our political system, and we should take advantage of that. But we need to realize that regardless of the outcome of any election, God is involved with the result, and we still have a responsibility to respect whoever He places in power.

A CALL TO BE MISUNDERSTOOD

In regard to cultural fears over the world espousing values with which we disagree, I don't think it's wrong to be concerned with cultural values that are in contrast or conflict with God's morality.

As a Christian, I believe God's way to live is the best way to live. I see God's values as the best values. I think it's dangerous when people promote beliefs and ideals that are outside what God has taught in His Word. I believe that because I think beliefs and ideals that are outside of who God made us to be lead to self-destruction and alienation from Him.

But at the same time, many Christians get so caught up in their fear over the moral decline of our culture that they can't seem to see anything else. It's as if sin surprises them, as if they don't *expect* people who don't know God to act and think contrary to how He wants them to think and act. More than that, there are some Christians—specifically Christian leaders—who seem to view the world with such negativity and hopelessness that they are ready to head out of here and escape.

In all honesty, I don't see things that way. Granted I'm young and probably naïve, but when I read historical accounts of previous cultures, it seems to me that we're a lot better off than most. But even if I'm wrong, even if there truly is a new wave of moral decline sweeping through our nation and the world, I still don't believe we Christians should lose hope and become fearful and downcast.

On the other hand, I think many Christians try so hard to relate to the world that they begin to lose their identity as Christ-followers. Over the past few years we've seen this a lot as various denominations try to respond to the cultural changes around us. I don't want to mention particular issues because our response to those issues can be extremely divisive. But I think we need to ask ourselves this question: Is our approach to relating to the world diminishing our identity as those who belong to Christ?

I think both approaches—being overwhelmed by moral slippage or diminishing our identity as Christians to connect to the world—can be dangerous because both ignore a certain common calling. You see, we are all commonly called to be misunderstood. Even more, we are commonly called to become fools—at least in the way the world sees us.

Notice the theme of "foolishness" in 1 Corinthians:

For the message of the cross is foolishness to those who are perishing, but to us who are being saved it is the power of God. For it is written: "I will destroy the wisdom of the wise; the intelligence of the intelligent I will frustrate." Where is the wise person? Where is the teacher of the law? Where is the philosopher of this age? Has not God made foolish the wisdom of the world? (1:18–20)

This is what we speak, not in words taught us by human wisdom but in words taught by the Spirit, explaining spiritual realities with Spirit-taught words. The person without the Spirit does not accept the things that come from the Spirit of God but considers them foolishness, and cannot understand them because they are discerned only through the Spirit. (2:13–14)

Do not deceive yourselves. If any of you think you are wise by the standards of this age, you should become "fools" so that you may become wise. For the wisdom of this world is foolishness in God's sight. As it is written: "He catches the wise in their craftiness"; and again, "The Lord knows that the thoughts of the wise are futile." (3:18–20)

The world is going to naturally do things that don't make sense to Christians, and Christians are going to naturally do things that don't make sense to the world. So we shouldn't be surprised or fearful when the "wisdom of the world" promotes values and ideals that contradict the "wisdom of God." And we shouldn't allow ourselves to become frustrated, dismayed, or discouraged either. I believe the above passages suggest that the perceived "foolishness" of the gospel will be one of the things that actually leads some people to consider its truth. It makes me wonder: Perhaps the greater the contrast between Christians and the world happens to be, the greater is the potential for people to come to faith in Christ

Maybe the world's moral slippage can further distinguish those who belong to Christ from those who belong to the world. Maybe instead of praying only for the promotion of Christian values, we should also pray that the veil be removed from the eyes of worldly people and that we can all see each other for who we are and who we really belong to. When we see moral slippage around us, maybe we should allow it to further distinguish truth from evil. Instead of being fearful or stressed out about it, let's use it to our advantage. This could provide a better opportunity for the gospel.

A CALL TO FIND SHELTER IN GOD

These are scary times. There is terrorism, rioting, police shootings, men ambushing police officers, and extremist groups in other countries who behead people and light them on fire. I can see why people are scared—I'm scared too! Yet we as Christians are called to not be afraid but to find shelter in God, especially when we can't help but feel frightened.

My little girl is scared to death of what she calls "the booms." Sometimes "the booms" are thunder, but other times they are fireworks. It was the Fourth of July weekend, and for about five days straight she would wake up terrified whenever

WHAT TO DO WHEN YOU DON'T KNOW WHAT TO DO

a firecracker or bottle rocket exploded in the distance. I would hear her screaming in her room, and I would run in to find her covering her ears with both hands while calling for help.

"I don't like the booms, Daddy," she would say. "Make the booms stop."

"It's okay, baby. They can't hurt you. The booms are just noise."

It didn't matter what I said, however. She was terrified, and I knew of only one way to fix it: "Do you want to sleep in Mommy and Daddy's bed?"

She didn't say anything but just jumped up in her bed like a cat that falls off a balcony backwards and lands on its feet, and she lunged into my arms. She was shaking as I carried her to my room and laid her in bed. It was only 9 p.m. or so, and I wanted to go back out and spend time with my wife. I thought that by laying her down in our bed, I could make her feel safe enough for me to slip back out into the living room. I was wrong. Being in our bed wasn't enough.

"Daddy, cuddle with me forever," she said.

That night I realized something: Mommy and Daddy's bed was a refuge to my daughter, but only if Mommy or Daddy were in the bed with her. It wasn't enough for her to be in a safe place; she needed our presence to feel truly secure and sheltered.

In reality, we can't help but feel afraid, even terrified, at times. When scary things happen—like the terrorist attacks on September 11, 2001, or a shooting at an elementary school—our natural response is to become scared for our lives and for the lives of those we care about.

Psalm 91 convinces me that God knows that regardless of

how many times He tells us not to be afraid, we are still going to feel scared sometimes. Just like when I told Ava that the booms were only noise, God knows that when scary things happen, logic and reason don't always work (in fact, they hardly ever work in these situations). So what does God offer? He offers us a refuge:

> Whoever dwells in the shelter of the Most High will rest in the shadow of the Almighty. I will say of the LORD, "He is my refuge and my fortress, my God in whom I trust." Surely he will save you from the fowler's snare and from the deadly pestilence. He will cover you with his feathers, and under his wings you will find refuge; his faithfulness will be your shield and rampart. You will not fear the terror of night.... If you say, "The LORD is my refuge," and you make the Most High your dwelling, no harm will overtake you, no disaster will come near your tent. (PSALM 91:1–5, 9–10)

We could reword this Psalm something like this: "If you climb up in the Father's bed when you get scared, He will put His arms around you and keep you safe."

Interestingly, when I cuddled up to Ava during the Fourth of July weekend, she no longer heard "the booms." Instead, she fell soundly asleep.

So when you find yourself caught up in the fearful anticipation of politics, the moral slippage of our culture, threats of violence, or economic woes, don't become dismayed or paralyzed by all the bad things that could happen. Instead, put your trust in God's presence.

There is one more common calling we haven't talked about

yet—and it applies to all of us. It's also the one I consider to be the most difficult of all. It's not about what to do in the midst of evil, but has to do with how we should respond to evil once it has happened.

A CALL TO LOVE OUR ENEMIES

I began this chapter recounting how both the Amish in Pennsylvania and the A.M.E. congregation in Charleston surprised the world by responding to evil with forgiveness and mercy. There's another example of this, and it involves an entire nation.

Her name was "Blessing," but all of her friends called her Alice. She was one of our guides and translators for a twelve-day trip to Rwanda. My wife and I were part of the Anglican Church of Rwanda in the United States until it merged into the Anglican Church of North America. Our church still has deep connections with Rwanda, even though the title has gone away. As a result of this connection, our church takes trips to Rwanda twice a year, and my wife and I were privileged to go on one.

Although we learned a few Rwandan words in the months leading up to the trip, you can only pick up so much of a different language without being in the country. As a result, when we got to Rwanda, we needed help. Alice was one of the people sent to help us.

Alice is a beautiful woman with a dark complexion, a sweet smile, and lots of stories. My wife sat next to her nearly every time we loaded into the bus to go somewhere, and she soaked in every story or detail about Rwanda Alice was willing to share. I sat next to my wife, looked out the window, and imagined Alice's stories coming to life as we drove through the Rwandan countryside.

Rwanda is known as the "Land of a Thousand Hills," and that is a fitting name. There are at least 1,000 hills in Rwanda, and regardless of which road you take or which direction you drive, you will go up and down and up and down. Because of the hills, the Rwandan people grow food in one of two ways. Most people do what's called terrace farming, which means they cut flat places into the hillside and do their farming on surfaces called "terraces." Many others farm at the bottom of the valley, where it is flat and there's a good supply of water. As we drove through the villages and cities in Rwanda, I was mesmerized looking out at the terraces and watching farmers in the valleys.

Rwanda is also very lush, especially in the valleys, where tall grasses and other plants grow. It's common to see cattle grazing or other livestock meandering through the valley. I wonder if God had Rwanda in mind when He inspired Asaph to write, "For all the animals of the forest are mine, and I own the cattle on a thousand hills" (Psalm 50:10 NLT). In Rwanda, there are definitely both cattle and a thousand hills.

On one particular day during our trip, we were driving above one of these lush fields, and we could see cattle grazing. The scenery triggered within Alice a story she hadn't shared yet.

"When the genocide began," Alice said, "my mom hid me in a field like this one. I was only a baby hidden under the scrawny legs of black and white cows, but my mom felt it was less risky to hide me in a field of tall grass than to attempt to keep me near our home. Our neighbors were going from house to house dragging people from their homes and slaughtering them on the spot. Women were being ravished in unimaginable ways before they were killed with machetes. My dad was killed. Over a million people were murdered in only one hundred days here in Rwanda, and I survived because my mom hid me in a field like this one."

I don't know how much you know about the 1994 genocide in Rwanda, but it is an overwhelming, horrifying story. In a span of 100 days, the Hutu ethnic majority in Rwanda slaughtered more than a million people, mostly from the Tutsi minority.

On the flight to Rwanda—a *very* long flight—I read a book titled *The Bishop of Rwanda* by John Rucyahana, a Rwandan Anglican bishop. Have you ever read or heard a story you hated and loved at the same time? That's how this book affected me. I couldn't put it down, but I also wanted to throw it out of the plane. It told the incredible story of a man who helped the nation heal after the genocide.

The Bishop of Rwanda painted a story similar to the one Alice painted. So much evil happened in such a short amount of time. Neighbors turned against neighbors, friends turned against friends, and family members killed other family members. One pastor invited the Tutsi members of his congregation—men, women, and children—to find refuge in his church, and he locked the door behind them. Then someone drove a bulldozer into the building, demolishing the church and killing everyone inside.

Interestingly, however, the story of Rwanda, like the stories of the Amish in Pennsylvania and the people at the AME church in Charleston, transitioned from a story of evil to one of reconciliation.

Rwanda invented something called a "reconciliation village." There were so many guilty perpetrators and so many victims of the genocide that the Rwandan government was unable to prosecute everyone. The prisons weren't big enough, and it would have completely disabled the already diminished country to have half of the population behind bars. They had to come up with a new solution to promote justice. And they did.

Many of the perpetrators who genuinely repented of their actions—except for the organizers and leaders of the genocide—were given the opportunity to leave prison and build houses for the families of those they had killed. After building a house for the victim's family, the perpetrators would then build their own homes next door so they could be close enough to help the family in whatever ways they could. As a result, several reconciliation villages in Rwanda were formed, and perpetrators and victims now live side-by-side as neighbors.

My wife and I went to one of these villages, but my mind still couldn't get around the idea of growing up next door to the man who killed my dad and brothers. Yet, Rwandans are living this way every day. They have found a way to turn a story of incredible evil into one of reconciliation.

There's a common call in the Bible that could be the most difficult of all, yet I witnessed it in action in Rwanda:

> But to you who are listening I say: Love your enemies, do good to those who hate you, bless those who curse you, pray for those who mistreat you. If someone slaps you on

one cheek, turn to them the other also. If someone takes your coat, do not withhold your shirt from them. Give to everyone who asks you, and if anyone takes what belongs to you, do not demand it back. Do to others as you would have them do to you.

If you love those who love you, what credit is that to you? Even sinners love those who love them. And if you do good to those who are good to you, what credit is that to you? Even sinners do that. And if you lend to those from whom you expect repayment, what credit is that to you? Even sinners lend to sinners, expecting to be repaid in full. But love your enemies, do good to them, and lend to them without expecting to get anything back. Then your reward will be great, and you will be children of the Most High, because he is kind to the ungrateful and wicked. Be merciful, just as your Father is merciful. (LUKE 6:27–36)

What Rwanda taught me, and can teach the world, is that even the darkest and most horrendous forms of evil still provide an opportunity for reconciliation. It showed me that forgiveness, mercy, and loving our enemies are possible, even after that enemy has shot your dad, raped your mom, and murdered your brothers and sisters with a machete.

What I saw in Rwanda—and what I think the common call to love your enemies is all about—was a glimpse of the full gospel of our Lord and Savior Jesus Christ. Think about it: What kind of faith is it that even our enemies can be included? What kind of faith is this that my enemies, even enemies who have taken everything from me, are not just included, but I am commanded to love and serve them?

To be honest, I don't like this common calling. My human nature yells out in opposition to God on this one. I don't want my enemies in heaven. I don't want those who do evil to find forgiveness. I want them to suffer. I want them to experience the same pain they've caused others. I want the worst for them. I want to call out to God and tell Him, "Lord, you obviously don't understand."

But God does understand. You see, we were all once His enemies, yet He reconciled us to himself (Romans 5:10; Colossians 1:21–22). God sent His Son to be brutally whipped and murdered by the very people He was coming to rescue. Why? Because God loves His enemies.

True faith in Christ includes agreeing with His complete gospel, and His complete gospel includes not only an invitation for God's enemies to find forgiveness and grace but also a calling for us Christians to love our enemies. This love is not just a mental acknowledgement that we are supposed to forgive our enemies, but it also includes a deep and genuine desire on our part to see them experience forgiveness, grace, and reconciliation.

If I am to reflect Christ's full and complete gospel, I, like the Rwandans, must come to the place where I don't just tolerate my enemies but love them and want what's best for them. After all, if God sacrificed His Son on behalf of His enemies, who am I to hold *anything* against mine?

And here's where I feel most convicted: If I can't tolerate the idea that many of my enemies will be in heaven, then I can't tolerate the full gospel of Christ.

This is another example of a calling that is only possible through the power and influence of the Holy Spirit. If you think you can pull this off on your own, then more power to you. But I know I can't. I know I need the full gospel of Christ to completely revolutionize and transform my heart before I can be able to love my enemies in the way God wants me to love them.

In other words, God help me ... and you!

IMPORTANT NOTE: I do want to mention that if you are in a situation of abuse or danger, a love for enemies doesn't mean staying in that situation. Seek help from a pastor or someone close to you who can provide a helping hand. I remember someone telling me, "Turning the other cheek doesn't mean you need to stand close enough to let them hit you again." Don't misunderstand this chapter—it's not about putting ourselves in abusive situations or submitting to evil. It's about our response to evil. So if you're stuck in an abusive situation, find someone to help you get out of it.

PART 3

SPECIFIC CALLINGS

CHAPTER TEN

A Word about
Specific Callings

Then I heard the voice of the Lord saying,
"Whom shall I send? And who will go for us?"
—Isaiah 6:8

At the beginning of the book, we looked at the emphasis individual Christians, churches, and Christian leaders place on being individually called to a specific career or ministry.

Although I think we spend too much time emphasizing the concept of "specific calling," it is important to acknowledge that God indeed sometimes calls specific people to specific things. So I want to take one chapter to explore some of the biblical examples of specific callings.

There are more than a few biblical examples of God calling people to do specific things outside of the scope of what we would consider "common callings." In fact, the Bible contains several examples of God giving people very specific callings. But many of these examples seem out of whack with the way I was taught that I'd be specifically called.

There are some examples of specific callings that lead to specific jobs. For example, many of the Old Testament prophets ended up spending most of their time propheting (I know, it's *prophesying*). Also, many of the disciples never went back to fulltime fishing after the Day of Pentecost. Instead, it seems that most of their time was taken up establishing and leading the church.

But what if those are the exceptions? What if the point is not being specifically called to do something but being commonly called to live a certain way? I think a quick survey of specific calling in the Bible may lead us in that direction.

At the same time, although I think most Christians are commonly called, I think there are also individual Christians today who receive specific calls from God. I don't know exactly how that plays out in individual people's lives, but I do know we have some examples from the Bible of what that can look like. I thought it might be helpful for us to look back at those stories. That way, if God is calling us to something specific, we have a better chance of recognizing it.

NOAH: Faithfulness, Then the Flood

Noah was over 500 years old when God showed up at his door. Well, I don't know if God showed up at his door exactly, but I do know he was really old when God started talking to him.

Have you ever wondered what it looked like, felt like, and sounded like when God called heroes of the faith like Noah to a specific task? Did God simply speak to Noah out of the sky? Did He show up in the form of a human figure? Did He knock on Noah's front door and then listen to Noah and his wife whisper back and forth on the other side of the peephole as they decided if they should open the door?

Regardless of the setting, regardless of how it sounded or felt to hear God's voice, if there's one thing I take away from Noah's story, and others like his, it's that most biblical figures were confident it was God speaking to them. There were a few people—like Gideon—who either questioned that it was God speaking to them or that they were actually hearing Him correctly. But for the most part, the Old Testament heroes—people like Noah, Abraham, and many others—were so confident that it really was God speaking to them that they simply obeyed when He gave them specific instructions.

Even though it didn't make any earthly sense to build the largest boat ever constructed—and to do it in a desert-like climate, no less—Noah obeyed God and did just that. Imagine being at the Grand Canyon and hearing God ask you to build an igloo for thousands of animals because a worldwide ice storm is coming. Noah was in a similar situation, and I can imagine him asking, "You want me to build *what*? Here? What is a boat again?"

It shouldn't surprise us that Noah obeyed, however, because the beginning of the story tells us everything we need to know about Noah and his relationship with God: "Noah was a righteous man, blameless among the people of his time, and he walked faithfully with God" (Genesis 6:9).

I wish I could take credit for realizing that Noah's story was just as much about the way he lived his life before the flood as it was his obedience to God's specific call, but I read it in a book. In his book *Me, Myself, & Bob*, Phil Vischer asks a simple question about Noah: What did Noah do with the first

500 years of his life? Genesis 6:9 tells us "he walked faithfully with God."

God called Noah to do a specific thing: build a boat and save the world. It wasn't a call to a dream job. God didn't call Noah to a career of building boats or working with animals. On the contrary, He called Noah for a specific purpose at a specific time.

But Noah's specific calling was only a small part of his life. His real story is that he walked faithfully with God for more than five centuries. It wasn't until somewhere toward the end of Noah's life that God asked him to do something that would make him the all-time favorite character in children's Bibles. But Noah's life was not just about the specific assignment he received to build a beautiful boat that would later be painted on nursery walls for generations to come. Noah's life was also about righteousness and faithfulness.

I think Genesis 6:8—"Noah found favor in the eyes of the Lord"—might have been what qualified him for his specific calling. In fact, that may be a primary point of Noah's story: God cares about faithfulness.

ABRAM: Called to Leave Home

A little later in the Old Testament, we find the story of a guy named Abram. While Noah's story gives us a little context, Abram's starts like this: "The Lord said to Abram ..." (Genesis 12:1 ESV). We don't have any clues as to the setting that surrounded Abram or about the tone of voice God used to talk to him.

From a literary perspective, I think we need to deduct some

points. Come on, Moses (most scholars believe Moses wrote Genesis), give us the juicy details! All we know is that God spoke to Abram and called him to do something very specific: "Go from your country, your people and your father's household to the land I will show you" (Genesis 12:1).

Now, it's hard for most of us to understand how big a deal it was for Abram to obey God's call to leave his home. In those days, families stayed together for lots of reasons, the biggest being safety and support. You know the old adage: "There's safety in numbers." Back then, if you didn't have numbers, your chances of being robbed or taken into slavery were *really* high. Abram was willing to do something you and I can't really understand. But he did it because he was convinced God had specifically called him to leave home and settle in a new land.

Notice that God's call to Abram was not about a dream job or a specific ministry opportunity. God called him to go to a new land where He would provide for him, keep him safe, and create a new nation of people through his bloodline.

MOSES: No Dream Job

Now let's take a look at the calling of Moses, perhaps the most famous man in the Old Testament. God called this humble shepherd to leave what had become his home, go to Egypt, and lead his fellow children of Israel out of captivity. Was God calling Moses to his a dream job? I don't think so. Moses obviously *hated* the idea of doing what God wanted him to do. Can you think of anyone else in the Bible who used more excuses to try to weasel out of God's specific calling? It's actually pretty entertaining to read the biblical account and consider the excuses Moses used. At one point, he's finally honest with God and says, in effect, "I don't want to. Please send someone else instead" (see Exodus 4:13).

I don't know about you, but the story of Moses flies in the face of how I understood the idea of God's callings. As I pleaded with God to let me know His will, I assumed it would consist of something *I* wanted to do. Well, that's only half true. Part of me was scared to death that God would send me to Africa or India—but only half of me. The other half anticipated a calling that I would ultimately enjoy and find more fulfilling than anything else I could imagine. After all, I assumed that if God took the time to tell me what He wanted me to do, I would be excited to do it.

The story of Moses should make us pause and think about what God's callings sometimes look like. His specific calling was obviously not to his dream job, and it seems that Moses would have avoided it altogether if God had given him a way out. But Moses was not the only biblical character to try to avoid God's calling.

JONAH: God's Runaway

Jonah ran away from God's specific call on his life. Rather than do what God had called him to do, Jonah got on a boat and sailed as far away from where God had called him to go as he could. It seems to me that Jonah picked Tarshish because it was at the end of the known world.

If you're unfamiliar with the story, God went to the prophet Jonah and told him to travel to Nineveh and preach to the Ninevites, who at the time were enemies of Israel. Jonah didn't much care for the idea of preaching to his own enemies, so he ran away from God. I'm not exaggerating. The Bible literally reads, "But Jonah ran away from the Lord and headed for Tarshish" (Jonah 1:3).

The best illustration of how Jonah felt about God's calling I can think of is this imaginary scenario from the 1600s. The English and French hated each other and were always at war with one another. But let's say the King of England summoned one of his wise men and ordered him to travel to Paris to proclaim to the people a way to put themselves in good standing with the King of England. The wise man wouldn't want to go for two reasons: first, he hated the French and hated the idea that the king would show them any mercy. Second, he didn't want to die. Lots of bad things could happen to an Englishman in France in those days, especially an Englishman who happened to be the king's representative. French officials could arrest him for being a spy and then torture him until he gives up what he knows about the King of England. So what does he do? He gets on a ship bound for the Americas—the farthest known place away from the king.

Going to Nineveh to preach was obviously not Jonah's dream job. In fact, it was the opposite of anything he would ever want to do. Yet God didn't give the prophet a choice. God goes through the effort of booking Jonah on a one-way voyage back to Nineveh—and not on a boat, mind you. He enlists the help of a great fish to get the job done. According to the story, Jonah was swallowed and brought to Nineveh in the stomach of a beastly sea creature.

There's an important callings-related lesson for us in the story of Jonah, and it's this: If God calls you to do something and you refuse, you will be eaten by a giant fish. At least I *think* that's the lesson in this story. Okay, maybe not a *literal* giant fish. But the point is this: Jonah's story shows us a very different picture of what it can look like when God calls us to accomplish a specific task. It shows us that God's specific call is not necessarily a call to a dream job or to a fulfilling career. Instead, God's specific call may be to something we don't *want* to do. And if we refuse, God may still do what He has to do to get us to do it anyway.

OTHER SPECIFIC CALLINGS IN THE BIBLE

I want to encourage you to skim through the Old Testament and look at the examples you find of specific callings. Sometimes they include a call from God to do something epic—like marching around a city and blowing trumpets until thick walls fall down. Other times, God calls someone to do something relatively mundane, like travel to a specific city and ask a specific widow for cake (1 Kings 17:9). Sometimes we aren't told how people respond to God's specific call—like when David was anointed King of Israel (1 Samuel 16). And sometimes people try to hide from God's calling—like when Saul played hide-and-seek with Samuel by hiding in baggage strapped to the donkeys (1 Samuel 10:22).

Each of these accounts gives us a glimpse as to what it can look like when God calls us for a specific purpose, and I think we should look at these examples when we consider our own desire for a specific calling.

The Old Testament is not the only place in the Bible that outlines various "calling" stories. The New Testament also provides examples of God's specific callings, and these too can teach us some important lessons.

What was Joseph—Jesus's earthly dad—"called" to do? Was he called to be a carpenter and to work with wood and stone? Well maybe, but that's not mentioned in the few details we have of Joseph's life. If we define the word *called* as God summoning us to do something in particular, then we'd have to conclude that Joseph was "called" to do one thing: protect and raise Baby Jesus, to be His earthly father (see Matthew 1:25).

Seeing as how Joseph is such an important person in history, you would think he would have some special training and maybe a chapter or two of the New Testament devoted to him. But he doesn't. We know hardly anything about the man responsible for raising Jesus from birth to manhood.

We know Joseph was from a town called Bethlehem and that he was from the line of a king named David (Matthew 1:1–18). We know this because he and his wife, Mary, had to travel to Bethlehem during a census (Luke 2). We know he was a carpenter (Matthew 13:55), and we know he was alive for at least a portion of Jesus's childhood. Everything else, all of the other details about his character and personality, is pulled out of the few references to him in the Gospels.

I think we can safely assume that Joseph was at least culturally religious because he traveled to Jerusalem each year to join the rest of the Israelites in celebrating a major religious festival (Luke 2:41–42). We can also assume that he was Jesus's legal guardian because most of the references to Joseph are attached to Jesus's name like this: "Jesus of Nazareth, the son of Joseph" (John 1:45). Other than that, we don't have much to go on.

Yet we do have enough information to conclude something

about Joseph: he obeyed when God asked him to do something. Very clearly, God called Joseph to complete a few specific assignments. First, Joseph was called to marry Mary, the mother of Jesus.

Now some of us may read this story and not understand how big of a deal it was that God asked Joseph to marry Mary. This was a lot to ask because at that time in history, women could be stoned to death for getting pregnant outside of marriage. And by going through with the betrothal, people could have assumed that Joseph was complicit in the conception of Jesus—that he slept with Mary before their wedding night. Joseph's obedience to God probably meant a hit against his reputation and probably included more than a few judgmental glances from people in the town.

Second, Joseph was clearly called to protect Jesus by moving the family to Egypt (Matthew 2:13–18). This means Joseph gave up what was likely an established carpentry business for a few years. It also means that Joseph, like Abram had done so many years before, moved away from the support system and safety of his family. Yet this story also suggests that Joseph, like many others, was not called to a specific career but to a specific lifestyle—a lifestyle of faithfulness to God and obedience to whatever He asked of him.

One other specific New Testament calling applies to our discussion of God's calling: Saul's experience on the road to Damascus (Acts 9). Saul, it appears, was already doing his dream job when God showed up. He was evidently an excellent Pharisee, and he was very talented at investigating and rooting out threats to Judaism. He seems to have received numerous accolades for his pursuit and persecution of the new Christian church. In fact, if there were a hall of fame for killing and imprisoning Christians, Saul would have been enshrined with the class of AD 65, along with a few Roman emperors.

In one of the few New Testament accounts of God's specific calling, He stops Saul in the middle of the road with a light so bright that it blinded him for days—long enough that he probably began to wonder if he would ever see again. But God heals Saul and gives him a new name, one that doesn't have all of the baggage attached to it, one that comes with a fresh start. Saul becomes Paul, one of the most famous leaders in the early church.

Yet even Paul's calling does not include a specific call to a specific career. Instead, Paul continued to work as a tent-maker in at least one city, and he may have done odd jobs in other cities as well (Acts 18). In other words, Paul's specific call to planting churches and writing letters of encouragement to Christians around the known world was not a specific call to a career path but a call to a new lifestyle in which Paul used his talents to promote Christ.

I share all of these examples because they have all challenged my view on God's calling. When I was younger, I assumed that God's call was to a specific job, yet in many biblical stories, God's calling is outside what the person does for a living. More than that, most of the biblical examples I can think of are driven not by the specific call of God, but by the character and lifestyle of faithfulness attributed to the person God calls.

I think our obedience to the many *common* callings of God in our lives is the precursor to, and may be more important than, the *specific* calling of God. And if we believe God might be calling us to do something specific, we should consider these stories as we analyze what we believe He is calling us to do.

So, has God specifically called you to do something? If so, what is it and how do you know? What were the circumstances that led you to hear God's voice and His call on your life? Whatever you do, make sure you obey! Otherwise, you may be poised to experience a very special and unique kind of voyage—a very wet journey—in the belly of a giant fishy.

CHAPTER ELEVEN

My Biggest Concern with This Book

———◆———

When I was a kid, my parents emphasized giving God money. Sometimes I liked doing it, but at other times—most of the time, in fact—I didn't want to. I figured that if the church could afford golden plates with velvet felt, they could manage to buy pens and pay their staff without my fifty cents or dollar tithe.

My parents taught me to tithe at the same time they taught me to budget. When I mowed the yard or washed my dad's car, he would give me cash. He would then show me how I should manage it. I had three envelopes labeled Giving, Saving, and Spending. We would take 10 percent off the top and put it into the Giving envelope. Another 10 percent then would be placed in the Savings envelope. And 80 percent would go into my favorite envelope—the one marked Spending.

At first it was fun to be like my parents and give money to the church. I really liked the free colored envelopes with my name on them, and it was pretty cool to sit next to my dad and put my envelope in the plate right on top of his. However, as I learned about the real cost of Legos and *Star Wars* action figures, I grew to despise the first envelope. Every dollar that went into the offering plate was one more dollar I had to earn before I could buy another set of toys. It was painful. But I did it because my parents told me I should and because the pastor would know if I didn't.

That's the real reason they use the envelopes—so they know who is giving and who's not. At least that's what I thought when I was a kid. Not only would they know but the pastor also seemed to really come down hard on anyone who didn't give ten percent or more to the church. In fact, he would usually emphasize giving ninety percent and keeping only ten. I guess he didn't have a mortgage payment.

I remember so many sermons on tithing and why it was disobedient and sinful to keep all your money. All of those sermons ended with a command to test God and see Him give you more money than you had before. It was a good sales pitch—give the church some money and God will give you more than you had before. But it sounded too much like a pyramid scheme to me. As I grew older, my friends and I had a running joke about "tithing sermons." If we were lucky enough to find out ahead of time that the pastor would be preaching about money (I think the church tried not to let the word slip out before the service started), we would skip big church and go buy sodas in the youth room instead.

The point of this story is not that the preacher talked about tithing—there are plenty of verses in the Bible about generosity and giving—but that it was a burden. I didn't like it. I didn't see the excitement in it. It was just another legalistic rule that kept me from having fun.

The teachers of Moses's Law during New Testament times were notorious not only for adding new commandments to the Law but also for placing emphasis on the finite details. In doing that, they made the Law a burden. At one point, Jesus called these men hypocrites for taking the concept of tithing to an extreme. They used scales and measures to weigh out an exact ten percent of their spices, but "neglected the more important matters of the law—justice, mercy and faithfulness" (Matthew 23:23). They personally took the Law to an extreme, and this legalism led others away from God. Jesus said of them, "Woe to you, teachers of the law and Pharisees, you hypocrites! You travel over land and sea to win a single convert, and when you have succeeded, you make them twice as much a child of hell as you are" (Matthew 23:15).

———◦———

My biggest concern with this book is that it will become a burden. I'm concerned that people will read it and then make a checklist for their lives. Why? Because that's what I do. I like "to-do" lists because they help me to both stay organized and to accomplish whatever I need to accomplish. It could be easy for someone to read this book, write down the common callings, and then create a "to-do" list. Unfortunately—or maybe fortunately—however, we will find that our list includes quite a few things we can't do.

There's one other common calling we haven't talked about

yet, and it's one that really bothers me. It bothers me because I can't accomplish it, and therefore I can't check it off my list. Yet, it's one of the most important callings, and I think it summarizes who God has called us to be.

In the Sermon on the Mount, Jesus defined this common calling when He said, "Be perfect, therefore, as your heavenly Father is perfect" (Matthew 5:48).

What? That's God's will for my life and your life? To be perfect in every way just as God is perfect in every way?

At this point, you could start to feel frustrated again, even discouraged. We've finally discovered God's will for our lives— His common callings for each of us—and then we finish with one none of us can achieve. We all know we're not perfect, and we know we're not going to be perfect. So how are we going to step into our calling if it's something we literally can't do?

I don't know about you, but this can take me back to questioning whether or not God is a good Father. In my mind, a good father wouldn't create an impossible standard. Or would he? Let's rewind a bit and consider our earthly dads. Would my dad—a guy I consider to be a good father—expect me to show maturity beyond my years?

Yes, actually. That's the point of training "up a child in the way he *should* go," so "when he is old, he will not depart from it" (Proverbs 22:6 KJV, italics added). If I *should* go one way, it means I'm not currently going that way, and I need to be redirected.

The point of discipline and raising kids is that while children aren't born where they're supposed to be, good parents do all they can to get them there. As a result, parental standards and expectations are always beyond the reach of the child, at least until the child moves beyond immaturity to maturity. Yet even then, even when a child is at the point at which we might christen him or her "mature," some of the expectations parents place on the child are still beyond his or her ability. For example, after thirty-plus years of hearing my dad tell me he expects me to be honest, I still lie sometimes.

Not only does a good parent set up standards that are beyond reach for his or her children, but the parent also looks for any opportunity to help the child hit the standard. Good parents don't set up standards for their children and then sit back to watch them fail. Good parents walk alongside their children for a season to help them figure out how to hit the newly established standard.

It's kind of like learning to drive a car. As of this writing, my kids are seven, five, and three years old, and they already want to drive my truck. I think I'm being a good parent by letting them get a feel for it, but you can be the judge.

We have a longer driveway than most, and nearly every time we pull off the main road, my kids fight over who gets to "drive." Don't tell them, but regardless of who gets to put hands to the wheel, I still maintain control. My feet stay on the pedals, and I always have a hand on the bottom of the steering wheel.

My seven-year-old can actually steer pretty well, and I haven't had to grab the wheel in quite a while, but even he is still being guided. I still control the speed of the car, and when he gets too close to the edge of the driveway, I slow down so he has time to correct our trajectory. If you were to ask him, he would tell you he realized the danger of running off the road and fixed it in time. He's proud of his ability to redirect the car back on the driveway. But I know that if I hadn't slowed down, he wouldn't have corrected in time. Although I expect more from my seven-year-old than my five-year-old, I still help both of them succeed.

What if God takes the same approach? As a good Father, God knows we are not perfect and can't become perfect, and yet perfection is His will for our lives. I'm pretty sure that's what *sanctification* means. It's a fancy word to describe something that goes from dirty to clean, or, in this case, from imperfect to perfect. Yet how can something imperfect become perfect on its own? It can't!

It's a good thing God doesn't leave us on our own. Look at 1 Thessalonians 4, where God tells us it's His will for us to become sanctified. At the end of the passage we read, ". . . who gives you his Holy Spirit" (v. 8). In the same way a parent puts expectations on his or her child, God has placed on us the expectation of becoming perfect. And in the same way I allow my kids to learn to drive, yet I maintain control of my truck, God guides us and helps us along the way. The Holy Spirit, then, is the invisible hand on the bottom of the steering wheel of our lives.

Not only is it important to realize that God is here to help because He knows we can't live out His calling for perfection, but it's also important to understand that He is always helping us. He knows that otherwise we will try to do it on our own. I know I will.

I've wanted to discover my calling for a long time. I've wanted to know I was doing God's will and pleasing Him. To think I have a list of common callings in front of me—a list that describes what it means to please God—is exciting to me, and I'm tempted to think I can make it happen on my own.

One of my biggest concerns with this book is that you will read it and place more pressure on yourself to live a better life. I know what it's like to search for God's calling and to want to please Him. In fact, most of us are searching for God's will and calling because we want to do what He wants us to do. As a result, it can be freeing to realize we already have the answer to the all-important question: What is God's will for my life? At the same time, the answer that offers freedom can then become an even heavier burden.

The truth is, most of the common callings we've discussed do not come naturally to us. In the same way that it's not natural for children to become the men or women of character their parents may want them to become, it's not natural for us to become the type of people God wants us to become. So it's a good thing we're not on our own, or the calling of God would quickly overwhelm us.

The common calling to sanctification is not a call for us to figure out how to become perfect but a calling to experience glimpses of perfection through God's grace.

Grace—the intense desire of our good Father to show us mercy—is kind of a pre-calling. It's the step we must take before we have any hope or prayer of living out all the other callings we've discussed. I would go as far as to say that without the pre-calling to experience grace, all other common callings will stay impossible for us to complete. If the will of God is for us to become perfect, something impossible for us in our current state of imperfection, how else would we be able to step into our calling except by His grace?

Brennan Manning puts it this way: "We all are privileged but unentitled beggars at the door of God's mercy ... every

Christian stands under the Cross of Jesus Christ, wherein we find salvation."[1] We are indeed unentitled and undeserving, yet through God's grace—His unmerited favor toward us—we can experience His mercy and find forgiveness for our inability to step into His calling. God is well aware of our inability to become the men and women He wants us to be, yet He still loves us, cares for us, and doesn't give up on us.

So if you have arrived at this point in this book and are starting to feel pressure to live up to a new standard, then you're missing the point. In fact, there's another common calling that reads, "It is for freedom that Christ has set us free. Stand firm, then, and do not let yourselves be burdened again by a yoke of slavery" (Galatians 5:1).

Common callings free us from the stressful search of seeking a specific job or occupation as the answer to God's will and calling for our lives. Yet if we try to accomplish the common callings of God in our own strength and power—forgetting that the Holy Spirit has been gifted to us as our helper—we will create a new yoke of slavery. We will create a new stressful search for help in trying to keep God happy.

God calls us to step into the freedom of living in His love as our Father and to experience the help and support He provides for us to become the men and women He wants us to become. That is the point of common callings—not just to do "God's will" but also to allow the Holy Spirit to shape and mold us.

N. T. Wright communicates it this way,

The challenge remains the same: to allow oneself to be grasped afresh, day by day, by the compelling love and radical agenda of the most extraordinary man [God the

Son] who ever walked the earth, to be sustained by his powerful presence, guiding, warning, consoling.[2]

As we consider the calling to perfection, and as we consider the chapters we've read, we should not allow the calling of God to overwhelm us. Instead, we should ask God to walk through it with us, to help us dwell in His love. We should each ask Him to help us step fully into His will and calling for our lives. After all, none of this is possible without the loving affection and guidance of our Good Father.

Your Job Doesn't Define You— Your Worship Does

I feel like I know less about God's will now, then I ever have, but I'm more okay with that then I've ever been. The further along the road of life that I get, the more questions I have. The difference between young people like you and us old guys is this, we've learned to embrace the mysteries of God and to be content in not having all of the answers.

—ROBERT BRENNER, My Mentor

Several years ago I met a guy named Robert. Robert is old— not old in the white-hair-and-glasses way, although he has both, but old in that he has a lot more life experience than I do. God has given Robert the kind of wisdom one would find in Proverbs. I mean this guy always seems to know exactly what I should do, and he has been such an encouragement and help to me over the past several years.

I started meeting with Robert because I didn't know what to do with my life—and because he would treat me to lunch. I couldn't answer simple questions like: What is my dream job? and What do I want to do with my life? And if there was anyone who should have been able to tell me what to do, it was Robert. But he never would. Instead, he would ask good questions and let me figure things out on my own. More than that, Robert encouraged me to stop trying to figure things out, especially as it related to finding a dream job.

"It's all about timing, Daniel," he would say. "Don't be so hasty. Just keep being faithful to the tasks in front of you, and you will discover what you're supposed to do."

If you are trying to figure out what to do, chances are you might be frustrated and discouraged. If you made it all the way through this book, you may still be a little frustrated because I wasn't able to offer you the exact answers you have been looking for. My hope is that you've gotten to the end of this book and realized something, namely that our goal shouldn't be to discover God's specific call on our lives but to faithfully live out the many common callings He has given us in the Bible.

I'm convinced of something very important: A job doesn't define us. In our culture, we tend to define each other by what we do. The other day I was at a networking meeting, and we were challenged to meet new people without asking the question: "What do you do for a living?" I wasn't very good at it. I tried to think of different questions to ask, but I was stuck in my normal approach to networking. I wanted to find out what someone did, relate to him or her on some level, and explore any ways we might be able to help each other. I was stuck in defining other people by what they did and how that might benefit me.

But jobs aren't supposed to define us. Instead, our lives are defined by so much more. If there's one thing I've learned from all the common callings we've explored, it's that my life is defined not by the quality of my job, but by the quality of my worship.

The call to worship is defined by a simple common calling: to love God and to love others with all of my heart, soul, mind, and strength. And yet I can't do that on my own. Without Christ, my worship is ineffectual. Without the power of the Holy Spirit, everything in this book is impossible for me to do. Which means that without God's help, I can't live out His calling on my life.

I have a friend who lives in Rwanda. His name is Dan, and he and his wife are incredible people. He's one of those guys you meet and immediately feel like you've known him forever. Do you know someone like that? Someone who makes you feel right at home? Someone you can joke around with and who gets your style of humor? Someone who is excited to invite you over to his or her home even though you just met him or her ten minutes earlier?

I had spent just a few minutes with Dan as he helped our team exchange money before I knew that if we had any downtime later in the trip, I wanted to spend some of it with him. At the end of the week, my wife and I and another friend named Justin had a day off, and we called Dan, who then came and picked us up and took us to an excellent coffee shop. If you're not a coffee drinker, you may not realize that coffee is grown in Rwanda. So I'm not being cliché when I tell you this was really, really fresh coffee. It really was an excellent coffee shop!

We were all interested in Dan's experience as a missionary, and much of the conversation consisted of one-sided questions as we picked his brain. One question in particular led to an answer that has stuck with me: "Dan, what is the biggest lesson you've learned in your time here in Rwanda?" I asked.

He didn't hesitate with his response.

"I've learned to redefine success," he explained. "When we moved here, I was caught up in how to prove to our supporters back home that their money was well spent. I needed to prove to them that our ministry was effective, and I began to search for ways to quantify our influence. Unfortunately, ministry here was very slow, and there weren't any good measurables to point to and say, 'See, here's the difference we're making in Rwanda.' At first, I was ready to abandon the ministry. It obviously wasn't working. But God had a different idea.

"God began to show me that success is not defined by the numbers of people we can influence, but it is defined by our faithfulness to do whatever God has placed in front of us to do. It's not about how many people we influence, but about whether or not we influence the people God brings our way. It's not about the number of sermons I preach, but about my faithfulness to research, pray through, and deliver each sermon that God provides.

"And if we do that—if we define our success here in Rwanda by our faithfulness to do whatever God asks us to do—we will not only be effective in our ministry but we can also be at peace knowing that we walked with God and obeyed Him. After all, isn't that really all that matters?"

As we consider the wisdom of my friend Dan, may we learn what it means to walk faithfully with the God we love enough to worship. May our definitions of success in life be defined not by the quality of our jobs, by the amount of money we make, or by the number of people we influence. But instead, may we define success by our faithfulness to do whatever God places in front of us to do. And may we not be overly concerned with discovering a specific call or dream job, but instead with faithfully obeying the many common callings the Bible teaches.

With God's help, we can!

ACKNOWLEDGMENTS

Thank you …

One of my favorite things about writing a book is that it takes a team of people. It would be wrong for me to take full credit for the work you're holding in your hands. First, I believe I received the idea for this book from the God who is not distant but who is actively drawing me close to Him. He's a generous God and He's not content to leave me where I am, but He constantly challenges my understanding with the purpose of making me more like his Son.

Intentional Christian is, at its core, a book that describes what God has been trying to get me to understand for many years—that He loves me and directs my steps. So I want to first thank God for not giving up on me but instead continuing to challenge me and help me grow.

I have a very patient and supportive wife who has been carrying a heavier load than she should have to. Not only has she helped me schedule and protect time to write but she has also helped me use our finances to support this work. More than that, she has put up with reading early copies of the manuscript and has allowed me to monopolize date nights with ideas. I couldn't have done it without her!

I want to thank my kiddos, who have prayed about this book nearly every day since I first submitted the proposal.

They prayed for Daddy to get a book deal. They prayed for Daddy to be able to write the book. And now, they thank God that Daddy is done writing the book. (By the way, they've also occasionally asked God to bless the people who read the book.)

Thank you also to the rest of my family: My mom and dad—thank you for your support and encouragement and for believing in me. By letting me work in the family business, you gave me a space to try out these ideas.

I want to also thank Angela, Brandon, Meg, Eric, Granny, Uncle Jimmy, Abuela, Dave, Jeanette, Tio, Drew, Vi, Micah, Maggie, Rina, Kris, Nani, Sam, and Ken Schafer Jr. Nani—the Dewar's taffies you sent me got me through the final leg of the project. Thank you all for believing in me and for supporting me. You have given me the space to develop these ideas; have questioned me when my ideas were a little crazy; and helped me become the man I've become. I hope you're proud, and I love y'all very much!

A very special thanks to Blythe Daniel and the Blythe Daniel Agency for believing in this project, for helping me put together a great proposal, and for supporting the book. I'm so thankful for you, Blythe!

A few very special friends also helped make this possible, many of whom don't know they were involved: Dr. Meg Meeker, Robert Brenner, Andy Andrews, Dave Yocum, Mike Segovia, Mark Weeber, Virginia Hollman, Edith Dotson, Michael Tomlinson, Michael & Emily Erb, Bishop Ken Ross, Rev. Kenneth Robertson, Lynn Ray, and Debbie Medford.

Finally, I want to thank the team at Discovery House. John: You played a major part in this project, and you believed in it before it existed. I don't think it would have come this far without you. Miranda and Dave: You both made this project better. Dave: Because of you, people have a chance to read and comprehend a very important message that we both believe in. Ken, Cathy, Denise, Meaghan: It has been such a privilege working with you. Thank you for your help and support!

And to you, the reader, thank you for giving this book a chance. There are a gazillion books you could read, and I'm very thankful that you chose to read this one. I pray God's blessings on you as you crack open each chapter.

Notes

INTRODUCTION: WHEN YOU DON'T KNOW WHAT TO DO

1. Ralph Waldo Emerson, *Essays, Second Series* (Boston: James Munroe and Company, 1844), 65.

2. Alvin I. Fine, "Sympathy," Poet Seers, Web.

CHAPTER 1: WHEN THIS WHOLE "DREAM JOB" THING ISN'T WORKING OUT

1. Colman McCarthy, "From Lafayette Square Lookout," *Washington Post*, February 8, 2009.

CHAPTER 2: WHEN GOD WON'T ANSWER

1. Jennifer Elig, "The Fulfillment of a Dream," (blog), WestBow Press, July 5, 2016.

2. Christiancareercenter.com

3. *Relevant* magazine, September 10, 2012.

4. Chip Ingram, "How to Land the Job of Your Dreams," *Living on the Edge*. Web.

5. Keven and Kay Marie Brennfleck, "How to Land Your Dream Job (Even in Tough Times)," CBN.com. Web.

CHAPTER 3: GOD IS ALREADY DIRECTING YOU

1. Similar phrasing in NKJV, ESV, NIV.

2. Bruce Waltke, *God's Will: A Pagan Notion* (Sisters, OR: Multnomah, 1995), 7–8.

CHAPTER 5: THE GREATEST COMMON CALLING

1. Elizabeth Achtemeier; Leslie C. Allen; W. H. Bellinger Jr.; Cheryl A. Brown; Craig C. Broyles; James Bruckner; Mary J. Evans; et al. *Understanding the Bible Commentary Series–Old Testament Set (18 vols.)* (Grand Rapids: Baker, 2009), and "One Lord, One Love, One Loyalty (Deut. 6:4–25)" The Bible Study App.

2. Achtemeier, et. al. "One Lord, One Love, One Loyalty (Deut. 6:4–25)" The Bible Study App.

3. Achtemeier, et. al. "One Lord, One Love, One Loyalty (Deut. 6:4–25)" The Bible Study App.

4. Achtemeier, et. al. "One Lord, One Love, One Loyalty (Deut. 6:4–25)" The Bible Study App.

CHAPTER 6: A COMMON CALLING TO LOVE GOD (WORSHIP)

1. James K. A. Smith, *Desiring the Kingdom* (Grand Rapids: Baker Academic, 2009), 37.

2. Smith, 46.

3. Smith, 37.

4. Angela R. Yates, *The Rhythm of My Day* (Greensboro, NC: Kindermusik Village, 2002).

5. N. T. Wright, *For All God's Worth* (Grand Rapids: Eerdmans, 2014), 11.

6. Wright, 7.

7. David Peterson, *Engaging with God* (Downers Grove, IL: InterVarsity Press, 1992), 18.

8. Wright, 4.

9. Wright, 4.

10. Wright, 5.

11. Wright, 8.

12. Wright, 7.

13. Peterson, 19.

14. Wright, 9.

CHAPTER 7: A COMMON CALLING TO LOVE OTHERS

1. Darrell Bock, *IVP New Testament Commentary Series*: "The Parable of the Good Samaritan" (Downers Grove, IL: IVP Academic, 2010), Luke 10:25–37.

CHAPTER 8: A COMMON CALLING TO LIVE INTENTIONALLY

1. Jesse Carey, "What the Bible Says about How to Treat Refugees," Relevant.com, November 17, 2015.

2. *The Freedom Commons*, November 21, 2016, Web.

3. "Sex Trafficking," *International Justice Mission*, November 21, 2016. Web.

4. "Property Grabbing," *International Justice Mission*, November 21, 2016. Web.

5. "Police Abuse of Power," *International Justice Mission*, November 21, 2016. Web.

CHAPTER 9: A COMMON CALLING TO OVERCOME FEAR AND LOVE OUR ENEMIES

1. "Amish School Shooting" (blog), LancasterPA.com, n.d.

2. "Amish Grace and Forgiveness" (blog), LancasterPA.com, n.d.

3. Mark Berman, "'I Forgive You,' Relatives of Charleston church shooting victims address Dylann Roof," *Washington Post*, June 19, 2015. Web.

CHAPTER 11: MY BIGGEST CONCERN WITH THIS BOOK

1. Brennan Manning, *The Signature of Jesus* (Sisters, OR: Multnomah Press, 2004), 14–15.

2. Wright, xiii.

Note to the Reader

To inquire about having Daniel
speak at your church, school, conference, or event,
please e-mail connect@intentionalchristianity.com
or visit:

IntentionalChristianity.com
Facebook.com/danielryanday
Twitter.com/danielryanday

Enjoy this book? Help us get the word out!

Share a link to the book or
mention it on social media

Write a review on your blog, on a retailer site,
or on our website (dhp.org)

Pick up another copy to share with someone

Recommend this book for your
church, book club, or small group

Follow Discovery House on
social media and join the discussion

Contact us to share your thoughts:

 @discoveryhouse    @DiscoveryHouse

Discovery House
P.O. Box 3566
Grand Rapids, MI 49501 USA

Phone: 1-800-653-8333
E-mail: books@dhp.org
Web: dhp.org